PRAYING THROUGH THE WILDERNESS

Seven Strategic Prayers
For
Empowered Living

By

Reverend Doctor
Mark W. Thompson

TABLE OF CONTENTS

Preface   2

Introduction   3

Chapter 1 Wisdom 20

Chapter 2 Strength 36

Chapter 3 Courage 58

Chapter 4 Patience 75

Chapter 5 Discernment 92

Chapter 6 Anointing 113

Chapter 7 Love 129

Conclusion 147

Bibliography 155

Scripture Index 156

PREFACE

"As my life was ebbing away, I remembered the LORD; and my prayer came to you, into your holy temple. (Jonah 2:7)

"Lord, the thing I feared the most is happening, I'm losing my joy." These were the painful and even tear-filled words I journaled the morning of July 31, 2005, as I reflected on the previous night's commission meeting. At that meeting I had been verbally attacked, misrepresented, and made to feel as if the inmost nature of my commission in Christ was disingenuous.

Committed servants who seek to live a disciple's life are subject to be misunderstood and yes, attacked. History records that One was hung on a cross for daring to be who He was. Yet, human as a Pastor could be, I was taken aback by this most recent volley. This confrontation—in addition to a series of prior toxic events—weakened me in spirit, and left me unable to grapple with the character and the spirit in which the words were spoken. After a restless night of prayers and tears, I awakened to the reality that I was in a spiritually dangerous place and needed help that *only* God could provide. I needed God's Presence. I longed for understanding, release and yes, I even desired vindication. But, what I needed the most was the means by which my soul would be fed, restored, and empowered; this could only come through strategic prayer.

INTRODUCTION

"He was praying in a certain place, and after he had finished, one of his disciples said to him, 'Lord, teach us to pray, as John taught his disciples.'" Luke 11:1

Anyone who knows anything about God and the life-transforming joy of relationship with Christ knows the deliverance, healing and peace that are a result of prayer. Prayer is that essential life-walk with and in the Spirit. In fact, prayer is the soul's entrance toward ushering in and knowing God's presence and God's indispensible grace in order to glean, capture, or even maintain a measure of joy in life. This is because prayer is hearing the mind and passion of God, acknowledging God, calling and listening to God, celebrating the Greatest Lover, and it is the soul's clarifying tones through seasons of joy or discontent. While Christ Jesus said that we can pray or "ask for anything," prayer should be focused and so specific in intent and direction that it not only leads us to greater oneness with God, but that through the bonding transformation of our will, life takes shape and indeed becomes living.

Obery Hendricks exceptional work entitled *The Politics of Jesus* makes a most interesting assessment. When the disciples approached Jesus asking, "Master teach us how to pray, according to Hendricks, the disciples weren't asking how to pray as prayer was a daily part of their lives and character, but they were asking what they should *specifically* pray for. Jesus responded by saying what we have come to know as the Lord's Prayer: "Our Father who art in heaven..." Jesus, according to Hendricks, was not teaching the disciples the (how to) of prayer, but more appropriately the teaching was a stance against powers or shall we say the governing authorities that ruled and abused people, to the point of having citizens bow before Caesar as if he were a deity. Thus, when Jesus instructed them to pray, "Our Father which art in heaven..." Jesus was making the statement that Caesar is not God, but God is God, He is our Father, and He is the one and only one that we pray and humble ourselves to. Thus, the teaching was a stance of rebellion but moreso a revolutionary rebuff against any power that sought to usurp authority from God, but in particular, it was a prayer of specificity.

In so many ways I believe Hendricks observation was correct. Though we do pray to God and though we desire God, too often we bow and make supreme in our lives who or what is neither sovereign nor Holy. Because political, social, cultural, environmental, and other types of corruptions are witnessed and aired daily on CNN, NBC, CBS, ABC and every other station that carries news, and because there are many Caesars today masquerading as: drugs, sex, personal prosperity, possessions, and jobs that are so profit driven that common workers are literally being pimped, and because we live in an era of unprecedented home foreclosure, AIDS, bankruptcy, racism and the list goes on, I believe that strategic, systematic and specific prayer for contemporary disciples of Christ Jesus has become of greater necessity than ever before. We (like the disciple of scripture) cry out

"Master, teach us how to pray;" that is, what do we specifically pray for.

As a Pastor who has recently founded an interdenominational church, led in the spiritual and physical construction of a former Church, risen through denominational ranks, and pastored a total of four congregations – two of which were termed as "first churches," (which means the promotion of greater ecumenicism) I have reached a point in my spiritual walk where I simply need *more* of God. With the responsibilities of teaching, preaching, counseling, ministering, listening, counseling (oh I said that already), arbitration, building, encouraging, community activism, interceding, marrying, burying and all the other responsibilities one has in pastoral ministry, I struggle like many who are too busy for revelation, clarity and direction through prayer in order foremost to draw closer to God, and to be brutally honest, to keep from losing my mind.

I don't know what you as the reader experience as part of your calling and vocation, but sometimes don't you just feel overwhelmed and even sometimes feel like you can lose it if the wrong drip of wind begins to blow? The urgency for more from God and the need for greater understanding and guidance through prayer was aroused or shall I say birthed because of my second pastoral call to the historic Big Bethel AME Church in downtown Atlanta, Georgia. Pressed with the joyful strain of ministry as well as a church financial condition that I had never experienced, I needed help not only to honor and glorify God, but also to accomplish the work for which I had committed my life and had been commissioned. The tasks at this new church I can say without reservation were much more than I expected, and in many ways they were unspeakably dispiriting at times to say the very least.

Have you ever been overwhelmed? Have you ever felt like you fell off of a ship in the middle of the ocean and the ship was pulling away and no shore was in sight? I mean like we used to say, "Have you ever felt like you were sho'nuff in the time of a storm?" The help that I needed could not come from words that merely said, "Lord show me what to do; teach me how to be a better leader; give me what I need that would glorify you because the task before me is more than I know how to handle," though that prayer is valid and has integrity. No, I needed specific guidance because the challenges before me were so enormous that at times I felt completely lost and even unqualified for the mission; have you ever been there? Yes, I am quite aware of the life saving promise from Jesus who said, "I will never leave nor forsake you." Likewise I'm intimately knowledgeable of the promise and reality that "all things work together for the good of those who love the Lord and are called according to His purposes," but sometimes, even the most spiritually sainted saints can have their saintliness shaken. The Bible refers to this kind of spiritual location as a "wilderness" or *midbar*, a place where cattle nor humans are meant to graze. By definition do you see the struggle? The wilderness is a place that is not suited by any sense for sustained human habitation or development, much less spiritual wholeness.

A wilderness for a man or woman is when your sincerest prayers leave you with red and swollen eyes but yet unresolved issues. It's a place where one struggles for insight and inner renewal, but in many ways the day or even days seem to progress with a growing sense of desolation and isolation. The wilderness is a place where you know that you are not only out of position as it relates to your purpose, but it's a place where there is no sure footing, spiritual equilibrium or even the aroma of peace. Further, the wilderness is that place where one's spirit is so parched that a flash flood is but a trickle of respite as it relates to the soul's and mind's deepest thirst. For the one whose home has been foreclosed with two young children, for the one who has no family to which to turn when the lights are being turned off, for the one who has been given the declining diagnosis but no means for which to pay for treatment, for the ones who received the call in the middle of the night about their child being involved in a wreck, these and so many other experiences and traumas of life can become and in truth *are* wilderness experiences where there's little to perhaps no spiritual balance that can come *but* through the power of prayer.

To the orphan who has been in a home for too many years, seeing one friend after another leave while no one even looks his or her way to adopt them, and the pressing question in their mind is "what's wrong with me?" That's a wilderness. To the spouses who gave their mate everything they had to give with unrelenting love only to find out that their mate not only has another lover but also has taken all of the money out of the savings and checking accounts, changed the locks on the doors and put a restraining order against them, *and* then these "put upon spouses" find that because of what has happened, they literally have no where to go; that's a wilderness. For the one who not too long ago got the job, recently signed for the new mortgage and moved the family to their new city after years of transitional living just to find out that the first round of lay off's recently announced included him or her, and now because the housing market has turned sour he or she cannot refinance their home and save enough money to continue living there because the value in the housing market dropped so significantly that the appraisal came in seventy-five thousand dollars below the purchase price. To top it all off, there is a new "bun" (baby) in the oven, all on the heals of their Cobra-Insurance coming to an end 30 days after the date of lay-off. This scenario can go on. What started one day as a joyful time, now just a few months later has become a time of desperation; a wilderness experience. Whew, that's a mouthful, but do you know what I'm talking about? Have you ever been in a wilderness?

A spiritual pause in the depictions provided must be inserted at this time. The pause is for those who know something/anything about the power of prayer, or who need to know prayer's power.

I am firmly convinced and a witness to the promise that "no weapon formed against us shall prosper." (Isa. 54:17) I also stand on the truth that the favor of God is both mysterious and miraculous, but it is *certain* and *testifyable* (I made this word up). Further, I stand in agreement with one of my favorite authors, Henri Nouwen who wrote: "We also need to remind each other that the cup of sorrow is also the cup of joy we share, and that precisely what causes us sadness can become the fertile ground for gladness when we recognize the *charis* [Greek for grace/gift] in it. Let us not be afraid to look at everything that has brought us to where we are now, receive it with gratitude, and see it in the light of a loving God who guides us day by day."[1]

---

[1] Nouwen, Henri. Spiritual Formation, *Following the Movements of the Spirit*. HarperCollins 3-books, EPub. Edition, May 2010. Pg.

The cup of sorrow – the wilderness – is a necessary part of spiritual formation. It is the cup that all drink from time to time, but it uniquely has the ability to till the soils of our hearts preparing it for the planted seed that facilitates transformation into the image for which we were created. To this, I, and I believe most of us can say, Amen. Yet, before the seed takes root or before our storm abates, it is while we are *in* the wilderness that the sights, sounds, strains, and struggles weary us causing us to uncover every tributary until we discover the "Living Water." In other words, while we trust and have our testimony about the faithfulness of God and the evidence that God always works things out, what are the aids/tools through prayer that will sustain us while we're in the midst of the wilderness journey?

In the time of the wilderness we need more than nice words from friends. In the struggle of the wilderness we need more than credit, marital, or psychological counselors, and we need more than Televangelists that promise ambiguous breakthroughs when the fragments of our lives are so dispersed that we wouldn't even recognize a breakthrough if it slapped us in the face. In the time of struggle we need much more than worn-out phrases that sound good when preached or when carelessly thrown about by those who for loss of words have nothing else or remotely spiritual to say. No, in times of wilderness we need direction that can only come through focused and intentional prayer. The purpose then for this book is to share seven foundational prayer principles that lead and keep believers focused and centered as they sojourn through the wilderness. The prayers and or principles are specific and intended to support and hold us in balance, provide buoyancy through storms, and leave us with that which will never fail us, hope.

I call this prayer devotion the WASACAPADAPAL Prayer. The pronunciation is simple, *Wos-Uh-Cop-Uh-Dopul*. Try it; you can say it. The term is an acronym, (not a good one I must admit) but it's what I came up with for the purpose of easily being able to remember the components of the prayer. The components of the prayer specifically ask and seek from God the following: ***Wisdom*** and ***Strength*** and ***Courage*** and ***Patience*** and ***Discernment*** and ***Anointing*** and ***Love***, get it? Though I no longer need the acronym to recall the prayer, as the components are now a part of my being, during the time that this prayer was developing I needed the acronym to keep me on target. Since its development though, I have found this prayer essential not only for my personal spiritual maturation, but also as a blessing to those who have heard me pray it in public or teach it in lectures. In fact, when asked to give the invocation at the annual Martin Luther King Jr. Commemoration, you guessed it; the prayer for the nation was the same:

> Lord, give us *wisdom* to see we are in this world together; give us *strength* to fight for what's right; give us *courage* to put away every anger and resentment that has lingered

and separated for too long; give us *patience* in order that we work for the good of one another; give us a *discerning* heart to minister to the needs of those who exist in the shadows of life; give us *patience* to not only care for one another as a nation but patience enough to put up with the many atrocities we don't understand that are planned and conceived by our brothers and sisters; pour on your *anointing* Lord and Lord most of all, help us to *love* one another as you so love us.

Don't get me wrong, this is not the perfect catch all formula for prayer – in fact none are – but I do believe that its components in specific contexts and venues speak to so many of our personal and spiritual needs. I offer this prayer treatment to you (the reader) as a means of moving you toward a deeper relationship and fellowship with God. I share this prayer with you as one that was pressed upon my spirit by the Spirit as one that can strengthen you through the complex and dissimilar struggles of life and prayerfully, even give you that "holding on" kind of faith that all of us need while in a storm. I offer this prescription for prayer as a means of soul support and spiritual guidance as you strain through the encounter of your wilderness journey. Further, I offer the writings to follow as a spiritual antidote sufficient for defense, intervention and even healing. The seven chapters within this book will discuss spiritual necessities for a whole life, and each, in their own way are purposed toward equipping and sustaining you through and even preparing you to handle your seasons of wilderness.

One final comment, it should and must be unmistakably clear that the heart of this work is centered on helping you the reader experience, yield to and embrace the presence of God while in the wilderness. The seven keys are also intended toward helping us realize that God is so loving, merciful and full of grace, that there's nothing He would not do for His own, to include endowing us with Wisdom, Courage, Strength, Patience, Discernment, Anointing and Love. This offering is not meant to necessarily withdraw you from the teachings and effects of the journey that you are called to make as a component of the will of God, but to help you recognize that while you're on the journey there grows within the undeniable capacity of *knowing*; knowing that you are loved, cared for, never alone, and that you will grow through the wilderness. Let me further say that though a life of prayer can become so self-centered that God's will and purpose are lost, be it known that conclusively, my prayer is that the leading and empowering you need the most will become clear as you pray through the wilderness.

CHAPTER I

-WISDOM-

"Most people don't grow up. Most people age. They find parking spaces, honor their credit cards, get married, have children, and call that maturity. What that is aging."
Maya Angelou

Like many of you I have the privilege of enjoying a career or a calling in life. Mine is a call to pastor and to teach. Prior to entering ministry full time I spent many years in the corporate arena, from collecting bills to selling copiers to management and more, and for the most part I was relatively successful. However, one thing I found was that the accolades of one's success given by others and or experienced don't always equate to contentment or that inner sense of fulfillment. Climbing the corporate or any other ladder can be a result of many things, for example good timing, friends in the right position who call your name, skill development, and let's not forget divine positioning. However, positions awarded or statuses gained are not always true indicators that one has arrived or one's true purpose is being lived, they simply and in many cases are necessary stops along a sometimes obscure journey. In fact, you may be one of those who are either at entry level or at the top of the corporate structure, yet deep within, as was my situation, you know that there is something missing, something needed. Don't get me wrong, I am a firm believer that God can take every position or posturing in life and use it as the prop that directs you toward your divine purpose. I am a firm believer like Paul who states: "All things work together for the good of those who love God and are called according to His purpose." (Romans 8:28, NRSV) I do further admit that there are some things or experiences that I would have liked to experience in another way or not at all because of the scar tissue that they left. Nevertheless, I have found that most of the seemingly worst experiences have blended toward my spiritual depth and heightening because I pressed to keep my eyes on God.

There is a truth that all of us need to emphatically recognize, that with the too often ambiguities of life, we need a guide which will keep us centered and purposed; that most necessary guide is called wisdom. Wisdom is a living organism that gives breath, foundation, development, establishment, and stabilization to its students. Wisdom is an inescapable necessity in order to gain a foothold on abundant living because without it as Maya Angelou stated in her above referenced quote, we are not maturing, we're simply "aging;" just going through the motions. Wisdom is not necessarily a result of pre-described formulas as in specific liturgies or rituals, but it shifts and adjusts with the movement and will of the Holy Spirit in order to meet each new need that arises as it keeps us on a divinely defined path. In fact, wisdom is a cumulative result as prescribed and dispensed through Spiritual engagement and life insight. If you are like me, you have long realized that simply going through the motions of life is fundamentally a waste of time and more importantly, our life is too short to allow time to randomly string us along. As a minister of the gospel I come in contact and conflict with people of all spiritual dispositions and needs, as well as demonic forces that drive me to my knees in prayer seeking God's wisdom less I am consumed or worse yet, overtaken. The immensity and weightiness of faithfully serving God, the call to minister to God's people in a way that helps yet confronts His people, the need to balance time alone with God while being stretched and pulled by all the complexities of life demands that I/we don't waste time, lean to my own understanding or even yield my attention to nonsense, but that I have an inseparable connection to the wisdom of God that fulfills needs. Therefore, the first component of spiritual depth and soul success that is needed in the wilderness is asking God for wisdom.

I fully understand the variable components of prayer that have been written, preached, and spoken about for many years, the need to adore God, thank God, confess our sins, ask for forgiveness, and make petitions known; those components are a staple for life and experiential encounter. But when

I state that the first ingredient of spiritual depth is attaching one's desire and whole person in God's wisdom, what we are asking for is the insight and way of God who is wisdom and who gives wisdom, along with the capacity to know how to apply it. How can I expect to love without the wisdom of how love conducts itself? How can I ask for joy without the wisdom to recognize the intricacies and formulas of God, which make joy what it is? If we ask for direction, wisdom must make its case. If we ask for healing, wisdom must share a discerning and providential voice for the occasion, and if we ask for direction, it is the imparted wisdom of God that distinguishes our desires from the will of God for our good and for the given situation.

According to Holman's Dictionary:

> "Wisdom is defined as: Three basic definitions of wisdom summarize the status of the field of study very well. Note that the first two of these definitions are quite secular in nature

while the third is religious. First, wisdom is considered by many to be simply the art of learning how to succeed in life. Apparently, ancient persons learned very early that there was an orderliness to the world in which they lived. They also learned that success and happiness came from living in accordance with that orderliness (Prov. 22:17-24:22). Second, wisdom is considered by some to be a philosophical study of the essence of life. Certainly, much of the Books of Job and Ecclesiastes seem to deal with just such existential issues of life (see particularly Job 30:29-31). Third, though the other definitions might include this, it seems that the real essence of wisdom is spiritual, for life is more than just living by a set of rules and being rewarded in some physical manner.

> Undoubtedly, in this sense wisdom comes from God (Prov. 2:6). Thus, though it will involve observation and instruction, it really begins with God and one's faith in Him as Lord and Savior (Prov. 1:7; Job 28:28)." [2]

Based upon the definition provided, wisdom can first be defined as what it takes to become successful through following predetermined norms of society. Secondly, wisdom is a theoretical discussion where variable influences debate the tools, parameters and measurements that define the societal ascribed definition of living. Yet when our request for wisdom is uttered to God, the prevailing desire and foremost plea is this, the *need to hear from God*. Seeking God's wisdom through prayer is seeking God. Without getting too preachy, if we can hear from God, marriages will be healed and saved; if we can hear from God, broken relationships will be mended; if we can hear from God, we can see

---

[2] Holman Bible

and hear the difference between loving someone versus trying to control them. If I may press this further, when we hear and embrace the wisdom of God, we will best know how to meet the needs of those who are physically and spiritually hungry; we will know how to comfort the ones who suffer because they have lost their homes during the most recent hurricane or from the mentally debilitating storm called foreclosure. With wisdom and I must say God's wisdom, we will not only speak against the evils of society, but we will stand prepared with solutions that begin a lasting healing process. With wisdom we will have direction and true leadership that permeates from the schoolhouse to the White House. And for those of you who are caretakers, shepherds or pastors, with wisdom we will know how to effectively work with the people that God has placed in our care as opposed to ministering to them out of *our* uncounseled, unhealed, and unrepentant mixed up mind set. Oops, I went there!

Asking God for wisdom gets even better, for wisdom draws us into relationship and even intimacy with God. Isn't that what the Psalmist suggested when he wrote: "<u>The fear of the Lord is the beginning of wisdom</u>; all those who practice it have a good understanding. His praise endures forever." (Psalm 111:10 NRSV) In fact as you study that 111th Psalm, you learn to give thanks, extol, honor, perceive and meditate on the providing hand of God because one has a healthy "fear" or respect for the Lord, and that comes not only through encounters with God but comes from the wisdom that only God can provide. It is spiritual wisdom when one transcends beyond the intellectual to the creative mystery and majesty of God and recognizes God's handiwork in the detailed texture of a green leaf. It is spiritual wisdom that not only recognizes the creativity of God, but also embraces God's designs as intricate offerings of love from a Divine Creator whose joy it is to lavish His beloved creation with expressions of His character and His love; that's wisdom. We see the sun with the mind, but we experience the sun with our spirit because wisdom teaches us that God reveals Himself in radiant majesty. We watch and hear the dancing of the oceans waves, but we experience through wisdom that the ebb and tides are ambassadors telling us of the constancy of His mercy and grace. We consider the movement of wind not merely in the sense of the humidity and barometric levels contained, but through wisdom we experience the many flavors of God's embrace through temperatures and holy conversations across our brow that remind us sometimes gently but other times forcefully that God's presence is everywhere! Yes, wisdom speaks of intellect, knowledge, discernment, and even maturity that are both mental and spiritual, but when praying for wisdom, we pray for more than those truths. We pray for a deeper meaning and even more profoundly penetrating bond with God and the things of God that ever reveal Him and expand our sense of being. We pray for the wisdom that transcends earthy ventures and operations so that we can cling to the revealing of

God's being. We pray for the wisdom that makes us smile at the sound of a baby's cry because we would know that it's an expression of God's redeeming creativity. And, we pray for that wisdom that says I no longer want rote, going through the motions religiosity, instead we must have interaction with the Holy; that's why we cry out, "Lord give us wisdom."

That's what Solomon understood about wisdom. For him, it was a part of life he couldn't live without. If you remember, Solomon was a young king, and according to 1 Kings 3:5, while he was experiencing a dream, God said to him, "Ask what I should give you."

Solomon responded by saying, "Give your servant therefore an understanding mind to govern people, able to discern between good and evil; for who can govern this your great people." Now get this, Solomon didn't say, "Lord, give me a plasma TV in every room with a matching DVR/TIVO combination; give me a seven figure savings account with Wells Fargo; give me a seventeen bed mansion with an indoor pool for the winter and an outdoor one for the summer;" I think you get my drift. Solomon did not ask for himself, but based upon the responsibilities and the calling that God had placed upon his life, he asked for "understanding" and "discernment" which are both derivatives of wisdom, in order to manage and or handle what was set before him. In other words what Solomon said was "Lord, *give me what I need that will ultimately give you the glory*." He was saying, "Endow me with what makes you smile and pleases you, for in that my needs will be fulfilled."

Even at a young age Solomon realized that the greatest gift he could receive was that which brought him closer to God, for in that closeness he would find his purpose and inner confirmation which ultimately would lead to his sense of joy and peace. Solomon in many ways was already exhibiting wisdom, but as the text indicates, because God was pleased by his ***selflessness***, God poured it on him such that none other could compare. In fact, scripture tells us that: "God gave Solomon very great wisdom, discernment, and breadth of understanding as vast as the sand of the seashore, so that Solomon's wisdom surpassed the wisdom of all the people of the east, and all the wisdom of Egypt."(1 Kings 4:29-30 NRSV) Solomon teaches us all that when God comes first, we aren't far behind. In fact he gives us a testimony throughout Proverbs, and in particular says, "Happy are those who find wisdom, and those who get understanding for her income is better than silver, and her revenue better than gold. She is more precious than jewels, and nothing you desire can compare with her." (Proverbs 3:13-15 NRSV)

James the Apostle encourages us to seek wisdom in the midst of trials and adverse situations in life. He writes, "If any of you is lacking in wisdom, ask God, who gives to all generously and ungrudgingly, and it will be given you. But ask in faith, never doubting, for the one who doubts is like a wave of the sea, driven and tossed by the wind; for the doubter being double-minded and unstable in every way, must not expect to receive anything from the Lord." (James 1:5-8, NRSV) Herein is a promise given, ask and we shall receive, not only a portion, but the promise says we shall receive wisdom "generously and ungrudgingly." So get this, God wants to give us what we need; that's so awesome! In fact when we ask for His wisdom, according to James we should ask believing we shall receive it because God wants us to have it. How many times in your life have you wanted to bless someone, but because they were too stubborn or prideful you couldn't bless them? Within the bosom of God is a gift, and yes wisdom is a gift. But there is a gift that the Almighty has with our name on it, and within that gift is not only an expression of God's love and a component of His agenda for the kingdom, but this gift, this inborn spark of holiness is one that connects us to God. Personally, I'm tired of going through the motions of holiness. I'm tired of lifting hands in praise only to get weary limbs because I don't lift with wisdom and understanding. I want to experience the fullness of God and embrace Him in new ways so that every day is like a new step in the birthing process. That's why wisdom is so important, because it reels us in to the depths of awareness that our souls are thirsting for and truly need.

Having stated these truths about wisdom, let's pray:

God, because Your presence is breath and life, I ask that You pour out Your wisdom within us because we want and need so much more of You. We realize that without the wisdom of all ages, not only are our souls and spirits parched and barren, but our best efforts become mere chaotic commotion. Lord, wisdom teaches us how to witness and experience You, but it also reveals how we are to love ourselves and treat others. Wisdom places a sign post before us compelling us to turn from dead end destinations; wisdom confronts us when we would

Wisdom through love!

lose our self in ourselves but helps us catch hold of Your life line called sanity. Your wisdom God, ministers to our soul like the sweetest of melodies ever composed; Your wisdom draws us closer to Your Holy presence allowing us to kneel before You to have life poured in. Yet best of all God, Your wisdom allows us to do that which pleases You, and in that pleasing our soul is satisfied. As You did with Solomon and with others, pour it into us Lord. By faith I receive it, by faith I open my mouth and it comes forth, by faith I not only acknowledge it, but it becomes me. Thank you Lord, in the name of Jesus, the living witness of wisdom, Amen.

CHAPTER II

-STRENGTH-

"The strength of the burden bearers is failing and there is too much rubbish so that we are unable to work on the wall." Nehemiah 4:10

At the time of my second charge as a Pastor, I was informed by God in one of those audible encounters that for me are few and far in-between that my "time had come," and I was to be transferred to a new church to serve as its Pastor. I knew where God was sending me the moment I heard God, but the congregation I would be leaving was simply a wonderful charge and spiritual location in which to serve. We had grown together as a family; I loved them and still love them dearly, and in many ways had become comfortable in the assignment. I have come to truly believe that ministry is many things, but one thing it isn't, <u>a work of comfort or a place of complacency</u>, so God said it was time to go. God sent me to a Church known as the Mother Church of the South in the African Methodist Episcopal Denomination, a majestic and historic house of worship. It was a church rich in history, beauty and tradition so that a man such as myself was staggered by the grandeur and immensity of this new calling. Having arrived there after a very successful pastorate at my first charge, New Bethel AME Church, I entered the gates of Big Bethel with thanksgiving, but also with a sense of purpose to do what God had used me to do at the church I had just left, spiritually build the Body of Christ. Please understand, by no means am I saying that Big Bethel was spiritually devoid, but of all things of which I am certain, I know that God uses me for spiritual development and maturation that leads to believers becoming whole through Christ. I knew without a doubt that God had called me to this church and to its people, yet I did not fully realize what God had in store for me and even today I still contemplate about the many nuggets of understanding God gave me from that assignment. It did not take long for this new church to begin to increase in membership, and for a new breath of ministry and spirit to be received and embraced by the congregation. Yet it didn't take long for me to understand the enormous differences between congregations and in particular the difference between one Pastor's calling versus another's. In other words, though the outgoing Pastor and I had the same goal of kingdom building, the methods and means of conducting kingdom work were uniquely different.

I entered a downtown community that was in the midst of urban transformation and renewal, and Big Bethel was one if not the central leader in that effort. The former pastor prior to being elected a Bishop of the A.M.E. Church was extremely proficient and diligent in business affairs and along with the membership was a tireless advocate for changing the landscape in order to improve the community and the focus of the church. During the many annual conferences I had attended, I would listen closely to that Pastor, Dr. James L. Davis, and would be thrilled by the enormity of the work taking place at Big Bethel along with the effort of its people not only to save souls but also to revive the community. Theirs was an effort that few pastors could mirror, and the plans laid were phenomenal in scope and in faith.

At the point of my arrival, the church owned a senior citizens home that they had constructed, owned several homes, had multiple LLC's purposed toward changing the conditions of people's lives; owned and was in partnership with a men's rehabilitation home, and owned a H.U.D. apartment high-rise that housed many but was in desperate need of restoration. With all of Big Bethel's impressive outreaches, their major venture was a partnership between a local entrepreneur/builder to create downtown condominiums directly across the street from the church. The church had intuitively purchased most of the dilapidated buildings on both sides of the street. The partnership with Integral Corporation and the combined focus was so that together they would not only change the landscape but also bring new life to a tired and worn down section of the historic Sweet Auburn Avenue in Downtown Atlanta, Georgia. This venture was purposed to build over 100 condos that would once again house and repopulate Auburn Avenue as a place of not only commerce but also community synergy and living. The project was powerful, innovative and in so many ways a sacrificial stretch of faith for a church that was bearing the financial burden of multiple community outreaches while barely getting by financially. Please understand, the vision, purpose and the direction of this church from its people and former pastor were extremely innovative to say the least yet financially demanding in scope; this is the church and the scope of the new work I inherited as its new pastor.

Having worked and thrived in corporate America for over twenty years in various capacities from entry level to upper management, I was quite familiar with large projects, managing huge budgets, and working with multiple and complex agendas at the same time. However, in the midst of the newness of this pastorate combined with the enormity of the task associated with management of the economic affairs of the church and its missionary work, I quickly realized that my best efforts and ideas would need a serious infusion of **_Divine Intervention_**. Each day I would rise early, get to work anywhere between 6-7:30 a.m. and begin a long day's journey that quite often didn't end until 8:00 p.m. or often much later in the night. The long hours were nothing new to me; I am quite mindful and familiar with the reality that to be a good pastor and leader and to be faithful to God that devotion and commitment of time and effort are inseparable components of ministry. However, and I am not afraid to admit it, deep within I sensed that I was in over my head with the magnitude of this new ministry. It's one thing to enter onto a highway gradually and build speed, but it's totally different to enter into a lane at full speed without the capacity or horsepower of immediate assimilation. Ok, let me say it in another way, it's hard to catch a flight that's already left the ground; ah, that's better. If you get my meaning, the work I inherited was so immense, detailed, and so incessant that after the first week, my head was swimming. It is not that I wasn't qualified, I was and I knew I was. In fact that opportunity was one of the revelations of that old saying that God will not put more on you than you can bear. Yet, since I knew in my gut that God had been leading me in a specific direction of spiritual maturation for self and others, the challenges of spiritual development versus the challenges of catching a business train already in flight were bound to clash. I simply could not see a way to effectively manage these two enormous and necessary challenges in tandem. Allow me to say it this way; God had been preparing me for a work that was just beginning to unfold which this new church was a part of. Yet there was an inner conflict; my desire to teach and grow others spiritually in a manner I was accustomed to and trained for versus the complex and diverse business responsibilities that were persistently and unrelentingly pressing me. The question in my mind was this, "Lord, how am I going to do both of these tasks with any degree of impact, integrity or even efficiency?" In fact since confession is good for the soul, I began to ask the Lord not long after my arrival and some serious bouts of dismay and confusion, "Why?" Why did you send me here, and how am I going to bear this load? It was in the midst of these pleas for answers that the actual development of the wasacapadal prayer got its birth. It was here that my new prayer life took root and gained its foundation with specificity. While my first request in prayer was for the wisdom to be a good Pastor and Leader, the second appeal literally pleaded for the strength to *endure* what was before me.

It's a scary but joyful undertaking in revelation to fully recognize that one's own strength for ministry or in any calling is never enough. I am a witness perhaps like you that real strength; in fact the only strength, comes from God. I have no doubt that every good thing done is a result of the Presence that makes all things possible. However with that being said, being reared in a culture and society where we are trained to believe that our best efforts will result in success, and buying in to the notion that my best would always be good enough, I came to a chilling yet wonderful spiritual crash when I recognized that my best was deficient at best. It's atypical and almost societally blasphemous to admit that one's strengths are nowhere near sufficient enough to handle many obligations and responsibilities. In a world in which cultural and social ascriptions assert and even demand that one be strong, self reliant, and proficient at pulling one's self up by one's own boot straps (I always disliked that statement; what if someone doesn't have straps or the boots to pull up), it's a radical departure of thought and even ethic to admit that you don't have the strength to handle a task placed before you.

That may sound like a logical statement to you, but at the time it wasn't to me. You see I come from a family of achievers from my daddy who was a very successful attorney to my mother who was a house-managing executive extraordinaire. My sisters are strong individuals as well as my brother, plus the successes of my corporate life indicated that I had garnered a degree of efficiency that should be able to help me handle any challenge, not to mention the fact that I was appointed to the "first Church" in the entire state of Georgia. It seemed unconscionable to me that tasks given could not be accomplished given my devoted time, experience and efforts, yet I found that my efforts were not good enough, and I needed a strength that I simply did not possess. In so many ways my soul even today resonates with the people of Nehemiah's time in that my spirit was willing, but my strength was insufficient.

I ask you, have you ever been placed in a position or circumstance where you knew that you had what it takes, but what you had wasn't good enough? No. Well how about the time when you got the promotion that you were sure that you could handle? You had prayed about it, asked friends to intercede in prayer on your behalf and even went as far as claiming the victory, but the moment you got the job you realized the enormity of the position and found that though your education was strong, your performance history was more than sufficient, you found yourself splashing in a sea with one oar and a broken rudder. To make matters worse, those who knew you got the job were boasting about your accomplishments, and those who were against your getting the position were talking all kind of nonsense against you, but now you had to perform, yet you found yourself in a position of total inadequacy. That's not you; well let's try this. You finally met who you thought was your soul mate. After a short courtship, the both of you agreed that you were right for each other. You completed the pre-marital counseling; the ceremony was performed; but no sooner had you turned in the center of the aisle to walk hand in hand as one, something that you couldn't put to words was all wrong. Now not even a month later, you found out that your new spouse not only had been married three times, but every one of those former spouses showed up in just about every conversation that you had as if you were now dealing with a schizophrenic. Not only that, but there was undisclosed debt that would rival the national debt and your new spouse still possessed spending habits that would make a shopaholic blush. Not only that; well, that's enough. But I bet that it didn't take you too long to find out that you needed a strength that was far greater than what you possessed just to keep you from losing your mind.

Allow me to take this one step further, you woke up one morning and felt a mass in your breast which you had never felt before; you went to school to pick up your child just to find out not only had they been cutting classes but also had been secretly wearing gang colors; you had invested your hard earned retirement in a company that was operating under false pretenses, and you lost every dime that you had so that now after 35 years of service you not only had to go back to work but you had to start from scratch. And, oh by the way, now that you are at retirement age, no one wants to hire you because you are too old. We can go on and on, but the truth of life's truths are that these issues can leave you utterly breathless, jaw gapped, eyes glazed without a shred of coping skills left and the only One that you could turn to is the only One who can give you strength to keep going. Honestly, this is really a hallelujah moment, or as the writer said: "not by might nor by power, but by My Spirit says the Lord of hosts." (Zechariah 4:6)

In this new charge and ministry *I needed strength*. In fact I now know that one of the reasons that God brought me to a place of almost suffocating burden was to teach me that even with the best of my efforts, there was a strength that could only be found in Him. (It's time for a praise shout again; Hallelujah!) Have you ever arrived at that place? It's a place where you discovered that in spite of all your degrees, all your years of experience, and even with all of the spiritual encounters and equipping you had with God, if God didn't literally lift or take the burden from you, you would be crushed by the weight of it all. That's where I was, I needed a strength greater than what I possessed, God's strength. In a very true sense it was a scary recognition but in the same breath a powerful reality check that led me to the conviction as the Psalmist claimed, "God's our refuge and strength, a very present help in trouble." (Psalm 46:1) It's God's strength that absolutely becomes our healing. It's God's strength residing and even brooding within that changes the discolored state of desperation to the character of steadfast hope and renewed confidence helping us gain sure footing. It's God's strength that becomes our equilibrium allowing us to withstand the pressing pressures of painful predicaments. It's God's strength that is our "refuge and strength," (Ps. 46:1- KJV) God's strength that provides vision audibly, God's strength that disables every demonic attack of inner fear and sense of helplessness that rises against us, and it is that strength and that strength alone that enables us to join in the chorus with Nehemiah who sang the "Joy of the Lord is your strength." (Nehemiah 8:10 NRSV)

In the Apostle Paul's letter to the church of Colossae, while he thanks God for the Colossians faithfulness, he further imparts a prayer upon its people. He says: "May you be made strong with all the strength that comes from his glorious power, and may you be prepared to endure everything with patience, while joyfully giving thanks to the Father, who has enabled you to share in the inheritance of the saints in the light." (Colossians 1:11-12, NRSV) Paul suggests that one's strength that enables him or her to be strong enough to endure difficulties with patience is a direct result of the enabling power that comes only from God. His use of the word strength has several meanings from the Greek text that are worth investigating.

Strength is the word *dunamoo*, which means to enable. The word dunamoo gets its meaning from the Greek word *dunamis* meaning force, specifically miraculous power, and dunamis gains its meaning from the root word *dunamai* which means to be able or possible. When you tie these three words and meanings together, God's strength enables us to do what we otherwise cannot do in our (oh so) limited strength. God's dunamai reveals itself at times with force that breaks through hindrances, people, and demons within and without that spiritually asphyxiate us, and in times it is that miraculous force that makes impossible circumstances become possible. God equips us to do many things on our own, but the truth is there's much more that can only be accomplished through the anointing of His strengthening power. Is it no wonder then that Paul prays for that kind of strength to come upon the believers of God? Is it no wonder that we like the church at Colossae should ask for God's strength in the multifaceted, spiritually demonic, tragic laden upheavals of life that we experience from time to time? So then, to pray for God's strength on a daily basis is a plea for the equipping of God that overcomes the wilderness experiences of life. Because strength comes from God's omnipotent power carefully and inseparably connected with His presence. Strength is that touch or shall I say anointing that transforms us which in turn enables us to proclaim with bold assurance: "I can do all things through Christ Jesus who strengthens me." (Philippians 4:13, NRSV).

Scripture according to Nehemiah 4:10 says: "the strength of the burden bearers is failing, and there is too much rubbish so that we are unable to work on the wall." In many ways this scripture was a plea for help, but also I have read into it a personal revelation. Not only do all of us experience burdens that are too difficult to carry without help, but sometimes the "rubbish" referred to is the rubbish that we either refuse to or don't know how to release. In order to live, serve, minister and glorify God we pray for the strength of God through the intercessory disinfecting work of the Holy Spirit to help us cast off the rubbish within that we have carried for too long, for it makes us impotent and incomplete. When praying for inner strength we must recognize that there is still some waste and yes even garbage that we need to claim as legitimately ours, and then we need to pray to God to give us the strength to endure as God purges our defiled temples.

The Word of God labels believers by many names: saints, witnesses, the righteous, ambassadors, children of God and holy among others. Yet, many of us have problems believing or receiving these designates as legitimately ours and that the predestined character and nature that God has intended for us is not only possible but also spiritually tangible. We hold on too much to yesterday's mistakes, missteps, and mishaps empowering them as our disqualifiers, which keep us from ever moving fully into our divinely intended calling. But in fact, it is these perceptions and shall I say lies that are the rubbish that we are praying for the strength to not only overcome but also release from our very being.

Hear this in your mind and in your spirit, we pray for the strength to believe that we are who and what God says we are. We pray for the strength to welcome with open arms that we are God's righteousness now and in the works. We pray for the strength to see ourselves not as perfect, but as the holy of God simply because we see ourselves under Divine construction with God as the Divine Architect. We pray for strength to see ourselves in the light of The Light who calls us into the light. And, we pray for strength simply because it is our hearts desire to please God and become a vessel fit for service.

The only way that I was able to manage my work at Big Bethel with any degree of efficiency was through a strength that was both immeasurable as well as limitless. And you know what's so awesome? I *know* that's where God wants all of us.

God wants us to enter that sacred space with Him to know that all things will not be by our power or might, but by His Spirit. It is God's strength working behind and before every scene of life by faith that gives us the abiding confidence that every struggle, situation, or shaky experience *will* work toward our good. Living in God's strength when weak is the perfect set-up for a walk toward victory. With this in mind, let's pray:

Lord, without a doubt we confess that foolishly we thought that we could do a thing without your help. We dared to look to our education, our friends, our perceived victories, and our accomplishments, even our support systems as the soul source of our strength, only to find that they and we came up short. We dared to give so little attention to You with one minute prayers always asking, but never listening for Your answer or even what You wanted to say to us. We've even engaged ourselves in "church work" as an insurance so that when we would need help, we would feel a sense of entitlement to Your blessings all to find out that we did not ask for that which was our souls unquestionable need, Your strength. Right now O Lord, we ask for forgiveness. We ask for an enlightened heart and mind in order to recognize that You are our strength, You are our shield, our defense, our stronghold and that without You "we can do nothing."

So Lord we acknowledge right now that we need strength to be holy, strength to be kind, strength to love when we don't receive love, and God even at times we need Your kind of strength just to love and forgive ourselves. We need Your strength from our jobs to our schools, from our hopes to our desires, from our thoughts to our deeds less we stumble, fall and don't get back up. Without Your strength we are not even a glass half empty, we're just empty. Without Your strength, we are in motion with no direction. Without Your strength, we are failure in the making. Therefore Lord, pour upon us a portion of that which is wonderfully and completely You. Pour upon us that power and presence which makes praise genuine and worship pleasing to You. Pour upon Your anxious children a strength that allows us to see You more fully. For in seeing, we become whole, holy and we are changed. This is our prayer, this is our desire, this is our need, and we ask it in the name of Jesus our Christ, Amen.

CHAPTER III
-COURAGE-

"The ultimate measure of a man is not where he stands in moments of comfort, but where he stands at times of challenge and controversy. Dr. Martin Luther King, Jr.

Pastoring effectively, with competence, with integrity and purpose is not only a calling and gift from God, but it is a vocation of yielding to the inner voice that demands courage. In fact, being a living Christian witness in times of unbridled secularity commands an inner spirit commandeered by an indomitable power called courage. While I am fully aware, as I'm sure you are, of the scripture admonishing us that "God has not given us a spirit of fear, but of power love and a sound mind," (2 Timothy 1:7, NRSV) when I speak of praying for courage, I do not mean praying against a spirit of fear, but praying for the courage to stand humbly yet with confidence while living as a the servant of God. I'm talking about willfully and purposefully assuming a style of spiritual conduct that proclaims openly and without reservation the courage to present one's self in a way that glorifies God as it stands boldly in opposition and even confrontation to principalities and every spiritual demon without and within.

One's courage is not measured by his or her ability to quote scriptures in the face of opposition, but it's the act of yielding one's self to conduct one's life in a way that is otherwise atypical to societal norms. Courage is the spiritual ingredient that causes one to live love and not just occasionally flash it in the presence of whomever and whatever. You know what I mean don't you? For instance, when you have been cursed out for something you have not done or been accused, lied on or just treated unscrupulously, spiritual courage is that ingredient necessary toward maintaining a standard of peace because you realize that God will stand with you in the fight, and regardless the outcome, His favor will reveal itself on your behalf. When you pray for courage you specifically ask God for the spiritual equipment to forgive in otherwise unconscionable conditions; for the ability to tell the difficult truth even though it will hurt both the receiver and the transmitter; for the ability to linger in great swells of tears with the mother who lost her child due to a tragic act of violence while not trying to soothe her pain with empty phrases that are more about your feelings than ministering to her need. This is the type of courage to which I refer.

The need for courage is so multifaceted. This blessing or shall I say this needed gift from God is a priceless necessity in the times in which this book is being written. America, just a little over a year ago, surfaced from one of the most hard fought and arguably ruthless presidential campaigns wherein a man of multi-culture and multi-color Barak Hussein Obama was elected as the 44th President of the United States. He not only took office—as is often quoted—as the first African American President, but also took the helm at a time when the American and global economy continued in a downward spiral unlike any time in history. Hundreds of thousands had lost their jobs, home foreclosure was on pace to reach one-million family dispossessions, and although congress having completed an unprecedented 700 billion dollar plus bailout on the backs of taxpayers helped settle some of the upheaval, still many people were struggling just to put food on their tables. The auto industry who indirectly and directly employed over five-million persons continued to keep its head above the bankruptcy milieu of business, and the healthcare of the nation was on life support system because the plug had all but fallen out of the socket driving many to bankruptcy because of their inability to pay outrageous health care bills. Right now the United States and the world continues to witness human decimation and genocide through bombings captured by live television, which incidentally was used to drive up ratings. Gasoline and heating oil prices are bouncing up and down as swiftly as an NBA player can dribble; retirees who thought they were financially secure are panicking due to 401K meltdowns and therefore are forced to reenter the job market because what they thought would tide them over has become woefully insufficient. One of my dear friends recently told me that at this point of his life, he would never be able to retire, only expire. Wall Street melt downs caused by corporate white collar crooks who cooked the financial books and then seized their stock dividends and ran, combined with food costs that have become astronomical to say the least, have made these times ones that are impregnated with fear.

A recent AARP magazine article shared the story of a senior citizen whose spouse had developed an advanced stage of Alzheimer's. Having used up all of their hard earned retirement to care for his spouse and provide for her medications, he was barely able to feed her with what they had and had to beg for food on the streets for his own nourishment. As he stated in the article, he not only felt embarrassed that he had to beg, but he had no idea how he would be able to continue caring for his wife much less himself.

I must take this line of thinking one step further. I just referenced that the 44th President elect was voted in to office and the man happens to be of bi-racial decent. His father was an African from Kenya and his mother was of European decent from Kansas. It is now a year and a half after the election, but haters and shallow living "knuckleheads" are still trying to have him removed from office saying that he was not born in the United States. Added to that, the cable media are flooding the market with talking heads that are promoting and injecting more hatred than knowledge or answers about him. For instance, when the national health care bill was passed at the dismay of one particular talking head whom I won't name, he spoke these words, "We must take him out." Now, where I come from and what is so typically seen on crime shows is that when someone is to be "taken out" that means the individual should be killed. Here's the problem. Even though this national personality has assailed a death threat agenda against our president, instead of him being removed from the media, he is allowed to continue to have sponsors and a listening audience numbered in the millions. Plus and even worse is the hatred and divisiveness that I contend is a direct result that continues to escalate. Most of this banter is nothing more than blatant racism.

Here's what I'm trying to say. This talk show host as well as others are themselves fearful and creating a state of fear about what this "African American" is doing and is going to do to this nation. The questions arising ask whether he's going to bring about the necessary change with relationship to the failing economy to meet the exclusionary needs of a few, or will he take care of his "own kind" in a reverse good ole' boyism coup? Did this election mark a new beginning where those who had always been in power must now surrender to the truth that everyone should have an equal hand and voice as is proposed and purposed in the Constitution? Has America's practice of back room exclusivity that meets the need of the privileged few been forever changed so that those who practice racism, classism, sexism, greed and any other ism that is out there, discovered that their mansions of supremacy and control are being eroded by a sweeping and perhaps even spiritual dynamic called change?

In light of these and countless other acts of what can at worse case be labeled soul violence, these are the times in which this world is in need of God's spiritual cocktail called courage. Without the anchor of courage, it would become all too easy for fears, doubts, isms and even a sense of <u>nihilism</u> to gain a foothold and get the best of even the best of believers. Without courage that God is still in control, that God still cares, that God is always aware, that God is intimately involved in the very intricacies of life's experiences, the testing, trials and tensions of these days could overcome those of staunchest faith.

As stated in chapter two, my pilgrimage into a new pastorate placed me in the position of handling multifaceted roles and responsibilities that demanded something in me that needed to be birthed and matured. In fact it was a dear friend who stated that in the new charge I would have to "grow-up" in ways that would stretch me beyond the seat of my content; and "Z" you were right. It's an interesting truth, yet one worth highlighting that even if one possesses wisdom and strength, neither will make much of an impact without the courage to move upon one's convictions.

Perhaps that's where Dr. Martin Luther King Jr. was when he pinned the statement at the heading of this chapter. If you have studied any of his writings, you will find his conviction and regard for moral obligation and theologically sound stance as to the inherent worth of humankind and the responsibility to ensure its full capacity for all people is necessary if the community and the country is to become as he stated, the "beloved community." Yet, where excellent penmanship and phenomenal oratorical skills end, courage must be the inspirational light in order that change and ministry can move forward.

Even though America and the world continue to experience a financial breakdown that is so dire, no prognosticator, prophet or priest can predict its outcome; this is not the time for Christians to become weary in trusting God. Even though the job market is tenuous and forecasts look troubling, this is not the time to forget that God has sustained us through greater difficulties and is more than capable of doing it again. And surely, even though a uniquely new kind of thinking man has been elected as the President, this is not the time to be afraid, but it's truly the time for Christians and non-Christian alike, whatever the color, culture or creed to stand together courageously and proclaim as the writer said, that "If God be for us who can be against us." (Romans 8:3, NRSV) In fact, taking the courage mantra of that verse I am more than willing to say, "since, God is for me, nothing can stand against me!"

Paul Tillich in is book entitled *The Courage To Be* inferred that courage is for one to live ontologically with an "in spite of" outlook. That is, in spite of what life holds, in spite of the turns and twists of trying to live, in spite of the signs of the times or even the finality of one's mortal existence, in spite of it all, we are still in the hands of a loving God. "Tillich defined courage as the act of facing up to the ontological contradictions of existence."[3] Tillich is correct, because if life is anything, it is satiated with contradictions and ambiguities, and it even throws in to the mix Katrinic like storms that leave people displaced and dispossessed. Yet, there is a faithfulness of God that always breaks through the shadows of despair; there is a compassion of God that reveals itself in the maelstrom's of our existence; there is a loving God that continues to tend to our needs in spite of our carelessness towards faithfulness; and as Catherine of Cienne once wrote, there is a God who "acts like He cannot live without us." Based upon these indisputable truths it is the very nature and character of God that draws us in prayer to seek a wholistic courage that

---

[3] Trotter, M. Dictionary of Pastoral Care And Counseling. Hunter, Rodney J. Editor. Abingdon Press, Nashville, Tennessee. 1990.

binds us simply because of our intimacy and relationship with God.

Therefore beloved, when we pray for courage, we are praying for that presence from God that gives us a spiritual lubricant called assurance. Without assurance David would never have faced down his Goliath; without assurance Gideon would have run for cover when his army was reduced to three-hundred; without confidence Noah would never have built an ark in the presence of scoffers; without assurance Steven would never have allowed himself to be stoned for the sake of Christ; and without assurance Paul would never have gone to the gallows to be beheaded while hanging upside down on a cross for the gospel; <u>assurance is the offspring of courage</u>. So then, as opposed to just asking for a healing, ask also for courage to endure the struggle with the ailment; as opposed to just asking for the lights to be turned back on, ask for the courage to see light out of darkness; as opposed to seeking financial and physical prosperity, ask for the courage to be grateful with the bounty that God has already provided; as opposed to asking God to remove enemies, ask for the courage to confront them with a spirit of love; as opposed to fighting battles that have withstood the best of your abilities, ask for the courage to release the fight into God's hands; that kind of courage is your assurance.

Yes, the ultimate measure of a man or a woman is not how they handle times of ease, content, or when there's a full wind unfolding their sails, but it's the courage to trust God in a storm. Courage demands that we see beyond the unsightly in order to envision God at work. Courage calls us to responsibly and calculably to address those who would otherwise dehumanize us for whatever reason, and to respond with uninhibited care and love. Courage insists that we have the holy audacity to believe as we said in chapter two, all the truths that God has said about us and appropriate them for living while at the same time refusing to let anyone or anything to sway us otherwise. Courage, as Dr.

King but most of all our Savior Jesus Christ revealed to us is being honest enough to voice concern, yet passionately determined enough to perform the greater good at personal and sacrificial risk. Can I press this a little further? It wasn't that God in Christ Jesus needed courage to die for our sins thereby securing every believer's salvation, but it was the courage of the Savior to have enough faith in us to believe that we would not only receive His selfless act as a gift of redemptive love, but that we would dare to respond by making our personal sacrifice to courageously live for Him.

Yes, we should pray for courage beloved. We should pray for the courage to stop watching and start producing. We should pray for the courage to stop asking God for signs and wonders but recognize that God has already provided every word, truth, and revelation needed, and what we can't see or hear we will nevertheless receive by courageous and expectant faith. Let's pray for the courage to bless at least someone every day, the courage to be a witness everyday, the courage to speak the truth in love every day, the courage to love the unloved and even unlovable every day, the courage to suppress and release bitterness within while at the same time praying for the courage to forgive self and others. Let's pray for the courage to defend right, the courage to tell evil talking heads and every corporate network that supports them that not only are they wrong for their divisiveness, but we're not afraid to confront and oppose their empty and twisted rhetoric. Let's, my beloved Sisters and Brothers in Christ, pray for the courage not only to make a difference, but also to like Jesus, be the difference. With these truths in mind and spirit let's pray:

Right now blessed God as we thank you for life and help beyond our imagination or what we deserve, we seek that which uniquely only You can provide: courage. This is not courage unto ourselves or one wherein we may boast, but it is a holy courage that allows and equips us to live in confidence, assurance, peace, and with a sense of joy that through You we become able servants of the most high God. We need courage to live the Christian experience; we need courage to stave off the fiery darts and arrows of disrespect, disunity, and the devilish schemes that always seek to throttle and even strangulate our spirits. We need courage Lord to love and trust You like never before in order that we can serve You with a determined and unhindered spirit. We need courage to live up to the divine purpose that You have steeped within us so that we may lose our senseless insecurities in order to begin acknowledging our personal calling and embrace it. We need courage Lord when there are racial tensions so that by confronting love we can quell them; we need courage Lord when any child is abused so that we might stand in the gap for them even if it results in us likewise taking abuse. We need courage Lord to love those who are not always lovely, to have mercy on those who have diabolic motives, we need courage to face our disjointed and sometimes dysfunctional selves less we succumb or ultimately stumble to the viciousness of past sins or future temptations. For it is through holy and spiritual courage that we treat everyone as a brother or sister. With courage we reach out to bless someone, anyone unashamedly and without precondition. It is with your courage O' Lord that we learn to be more of who You created us to be, vessels that are blessed of the Lord and highly favored. Hear our prayers God. Give us courage in the name of the blessed redeemer who revealed to Your creation how to overcome every fearful circumstance that life could ever offer, and even how to overcome the fear of death. It is as always in the name that is power, joy, love, and courage that we pray, in Christ Jesus' name, Amen.

CHAPTER IV

-PATIENCE-

"May you be made strong with all the strength that comes from his glorious power, and may you be prepared to endure everything with patience, while joyfully giving thanks to the Father who has enabled you to share in the inheritance of the saints in the light."
Colossians 1:11-12

For many years and I no doubt believe for many to come, my favorite passage from the Bible has been, "Therefore, my beloved, be steadfast, immovable, always excelling in the work of the Lord, because you know that in the Lord your labor is not in vain." (1Corinthians 15:58, NRSV) The passage comes from the discourse of Paul to the church of Corinth regarding what happens at death but more specifically what to do until the time that ones work is completed on this side of life. For me the passage speaks about more than an apocalyptic expectation, it speaks to one's inner passion and conviction to serve, minister and sacrifice, while refusing to be persuaded from ones goals or intended purpose. The passage tells us to never stop fighting for what we believe is the will of God for our life even though the journey in the wilderness can become cold, bitter and even barren. Further, it's just one of those scriptures that gives you a sense of comfort and assurance that centers you against every *whatever* that may come in life. Eugene Peterson's translation of that same passage in *The Message* says it so uniquely. He writes: "With all this going for us, my dear, dear friends, stand your ground. And don't hold back. Throw yourselves into the work of the Master, confident that nothing you do for him is a waste of time or effort." In so many ways this passage alludes to a definitive holy destination for the soul while it lights a path for living, but it also speaks in broad strokes to the call for patience.

Paul provides a very similar admonition to the church of Colossae where he tells them: "May you be made strong with all the strength that comes from his glorious power, and may you be prepared to endure everything with patience, while joyfully giving thanks to the Father who has enabled you to share in the inheritance of the saints in the light."

(Colossians 1:11-12, NRSV) Again, from *The Message* the passage is translated: "We pray that you'll have the strength to stick it out over the long haul-not the grim strength of gritting your teeth but the glory-strength God gives. It is strength that endures the unendurable and spills over into joy, thanking the Father who makes us strong enough to take part in everything bright and beautiful that he has for us." That's the key to patience; knowing that in spite of anything, everything will work out according to God's will for His glory and for our good. Patience believes with the eye of the spirit that what seems impossible or improbable is but a favor away. But then patience, spiritual patience I might add, is not only actively waiting, but also doing so with the smile of knowing.

In this day and culture in which most activities are done in a hurry, patience is a necessity. In many ways to live and embrace this existence to its fullest potential, one must learn to abide in the spiritual scale called patience. Patience produces not only a

Patience mature mind and spirit through the growth process called difficult times, but patience generates spiritual, physical, and emotional depth of character. For instance, we need patience to be a good friend. Good friends are patient enough to listen to, cry with, walk through and even struggle with the friend who has needs without the need to say, "It's time for you to get over it," or to become judgmentally critical. Surely everyone knows, especially those who are caregivers, that patience is needed with those who are enduring Alzheimer's or what's referred to as the long sleep, or those who are terminally ill. Though patience can be a most burdensome journey for anyone, especially the one who is sick and dying, patience is necessary for the survivor or caretaker through the weeks and even months of ministering to the one who is dying in order to grasp hold of uncharted expressions of life that will teach him or her how to experience the loss of a loved one. In the episode and various expressions of death, lessons learned by those who are the grieving survivors will become fresh light when they trust that through patience they will experience a new grace, and yes even become greater aware of the mercy of death. Indeed where patience is at work, the survivors will learn new meanings and ways of living in order that they will not merely exist in the quandary of loss. Patience as strange as it may seem in this instance is the master instructor that will help both the dying and the survivor *grow* through and not *go* through life.

Patience is needed in marriages, and anyone who has ever been married should be saying right now, "I know that's right." Patience in the initial years of marriage is essential to secondary and third levels of foundation building. By this I mean that during the courtship phases, love, infatuation, sexual interests and even adoration is so heightened that quite often both parties will totally overlook each other's character anomalies, dysfunctional traits and dare I say pathological tendencies. However once the marriage takes place and the couple no longer goes to their own homes or apartments after an argument but are made to stay in the same place to work it out, without patience, the marriage is headed for the side of a cliff. Likewise with couples that have been married for many years, the need for patience is still critical and maybe even more critical than ever before. Now you might be saying, if a couple were married for many years why is patience still needed; they already know everything about each other? Well that's true but in many ways it isn't. As humans and as Christians we are constantly under *Growth* spiritual construction. We are growing, being challenged, enduring life altering tsunami's, experiencing physiological and biological changes in aging bodies/minds that we don't quite understand or sometimes are unwilling to accept. When you combine all these and so many more dynamics to a couple's life, if there is not a well-rooted subsystem of love, grace, mercy *and* patience, these marriages can become battlegrounds of discontent. Therefore like the newly married couple, those who have been married for many years need patience to endure their spouse's changes, (mental, physical, sexual, spiritual), their new desires, their unlived fantasies which may increasingly and grudgingly be slipping away as the days pass them by. But even moreso, it's because they know their partner so well that they need an extra portion of Godly patience in order to gather new thoughts and tools by which to help minister to and love their partner into new experiences and intimacies.

It's like this; seasoned couples know each other's habits, tendencies and styles of handling situations. But if the marriage is to continue on the path of growth and nurturing mutuality, the need increases for patience that will allow the couple's to see each other through the eyes and character of love versus simply seeing their mates with "*another issue*" with which they must deal. Let me say it this way, having been married for thirty-four years at the time of this writing, it is not easy for my wife to put up with my changing disposition due to age, job, the ministry or whatever challenges I am going through as a man and or as a pastor; heck it's hard for me to put up with myself sometimes. Her responsibility becomes (and I only say responsibility because "love is patient"), but her responsibility becomes out of necessity to try and find new ways to be a helpmate or the better term "partner" while I am struggling with what I may not understand myself. Her patience must look to God first and then to her indwelling gifts and wisdom as her source of guidance, comfort, inspiration, and assurance. She must patiently trust that God will develop in her the balm necessary for her husband in a way that will assist him though his crisis (for lack of a better word), and if not, have the same trust that if she can do nothing at all, she will have the patience in knowing that God will work it out. Of course this works both ways for as she evolves so must I, and likewise I must lean on this virtue known as patience.

Patience according to one author is: "An active endurance of opposition, not a passive resignation.

Patience is endurance, steadfastness, long-suffering and forbearance."[4] Based upon this definition, whether it is patience to endure a broken economy where one has lost his or her job as well as his or her pension, patience for a child that is intent on abandoning all the training received from loving parents, patience for the return visit to the doctor to discuss abnormal blood results, or patience for enduring relationships. Without spiritual patience as an asset, living can become utterly coarse. In fact by definition, patience is not simply waiting until, but it is actively engaging and striving forward with a confident expectation of the outcome. Patience takes the stance that no matter how long the situation takes, one is covered because of the unrelenting care of God.

Again, Paul states to the Church at Colossae that patience is the medium that helps people bear "good fruit" in the time of stress and or traumas of life. The Church to which Paul wrote was a newly

---

[4] McWilliams, Warren. Quick Verse Media, Version 5.0, 2005.

converted people to Christianity. The city of Colossae itself was considered a second-rate market city as it was overshadowed by the cities of Ephesus and Laodicea regarding trade. Therefore, because of its status and because it chose the Christian way as taught by an Evangelist by the name of Epaphras, it was important for Paul to encourage the people to stand firm in their faith, and to be patient against the attacks that came against them. Today in 2011 Christians and non-Christians alike are under great stress. Like the people of Colossae, we are compelled to deal with many contemptible and growing issues: terrible unemployment, crime, homelessness, drug abuse and a beast that has affected the vast majority of middle and lower economic classes, ***greed***. The bitter reality of greed is how a select selfish few have so demonstratively and criminally crippled so many individuals and catapulted this nation and this world into a deplorable state of nihilism. Right now America is experiencing great outbreaks of depression, suicide, purchases of guns with the permits to carry them anywhere and anytime, health issues, domestic violence, divorce, a rise in the general sense of the loss of personal well-being and, sadly, a desperate outlook on the future.

When people are going hungry, lights are being turned off, bankruptcy has become the last and only alternative, prescriptions cannot be afforded even with insurance, the electric is due but the food pantry is bare, and even the churches are closing their doors earlier or altogether because of the desperate condition of the economy, all these occurrences are catalysts that work toward causing heightened degrees of anxiety and restlessness. The questions that quite naturally come to mind are: am I next to be laid off? Will I lose my home? Will we have enough to eat? Should I put in an extra hour at work above and beyond the ten or twelve hour days I'm already working, and forget that I'm only being paid for eight, or very simply stated, am I the next statistic for something that is *completely out of my control*? These are the questions and the realities that many are facing today including myself, and the reason why patiently trusting in God is so necessary.

This is not a patience calling for a ship to ride through the flood, which certainly would be a good thing if the water was about to overtake us, but this is a patience and even trust that will unequivocally say "Lord, *whatever* comes I have no doubt because I trust You." You see, the patience or trust that I am interested in is the one that says yes, these toxic truths of life are taking place all around and to me, but I will not sit idle and become a victim, I trust God. Therefore, though some breathtakingly sad events are taking place, I will fight for that next breath of abundant living as I trust God. Though what I had always prayed would never happen just did, I will be patient enough to see through this mental and spiritual mudslide that when the mess stops flowing I will still be in God's hands and God will work it all out.

Patience then and why we should pray for a mind and spirit of patience is intended as an issue of *trusting God*. The words trust and patience are in a real sense interchangeable. I believe that's what Paul's message was for the churches at Corinth and Colossae, that they/we would be endued with such trust in our God that it would result in a mind and spirit of stubborn expectancy and not passivity. Further, that we as those who trust in God will not just "wait on the Lord" but that we will strive with a spirit of favored confidence because we are "of good courage." With this patience we may have to tolerate, but we refuse to stagnate; we may be delayed, but we will not be denied; we may have to accept an ill treatment or result, but it's only for a season because we are patient enough to know and to trust that God will and has already worked it out. As scripture admonishes us, "As God's chosen ones, holy and beloved, clothe yourselves with compassion, kindness, humility, meekness, and patience." (Colossians 3:12) To be "clothed" in patience then means to not only seek patience

Clothed in Patience

through prayer but to place it on as our garment of both defense and offense which are both held tightly to with unyielding assurance. Patience shows gratitude for the many blessings already received, acknowledges the Presence of Holiness that never departs, reveals a hope that enlivens the worst case scenario, and it causes us to *live* each moment of life versus running to live in the tomorrows that have yet to arrive and which may bring a whole new set of problems.

Throughout history we have witnessed the enduring patience of God toward His creation; now that's a powerful statement and truth. From Israel turning to idols through their being freed from bondage and daring to suggest they return to the same; through the unscrupulous ways in which Jacob would act and treat his own kindred, through the ups and downs of a "man after God's own heart" in the person of the adulterer and murderer named David, through the aggressive and impulsive attitudes of Peter to the one time person name Saul who persecuted Christians, God has revealed over and over his patience toward us. But we can't stop there, Look at God's patience toward us. From the empty pews on Sunday because tailgating took center stage, from the empty seats at mid-week Bible study because we didn't want to miss *American Idol*, from giving more money on season tickets than toward the ministry of God's church, from knowing better and doing the exact opposite, you get the picture. God has been patient with us. As Peter would declare, "regard the patience of our Lord as salvation." (2 Peter 3:15) With this kind of friend and savior, how can we help but trust Him and watch patiently for Him? God so loves us that God's patience for us is beyond our comprehension as truly it has proven that it has no seeming end. How can we then not ask for a spirit of patience? With these truths let's pray:

Lord, today we pray for a spirit of patience and the confidence that comes through patience. It is a patience not so we can simply get through a dark time, but a patience that will give us unfailing trust as we grow through it until the light of new meaning and even maturity is revealed. This patience "Lord" we realize draws us closer to You; it causes us to release our trained tendencies and inclinations toward anxiety and worry, as it draws our very being solely into Your most compassionate arms. Father, with patience, we will lay hold to every promise that You have spoken into our spirits. With patience, we will see beyond physical sight to envision that You are at work even when it seems that Your voice is quiet. With patience "God" we lose the need to run at a pace that only leads to weary legs and a broken heart. With patience we shall sometimes sit quietly yet other times run with ordained authority the course predestined for us, for we know without even knowing how we know, but we know that the whatever's in life will draw us one step closer to understanding, transformation, and the divine image we shall be.

Right now "Lord" we thank You for the patience that becomes the forerunner to our smile; we thank You for the patience that allows us to walk upright with a hand extended toward Your high merit; we thank You for the patience that causes us to yield the desires of our flesh as they get in the way of our spirit, and we thank You for a patience that reveals a living testimony in our undying trust in You. Shower then upon us "Lord" by Your Spirit of patience, one that is akin to that which You show us every day. We love You "Lord," we need You "Lord, "we look to you O' God as we walk by patience in Your sight; Amen.

CHAPTER V
-DISCERNMENT-

"Do not be conformed to this world, but be transformed by the renewing of your minds, so that you may discern what is the will of God— what is good and acceptable and perfect." Romans 12:2

As a Pastor who is committed and passionate about being a good shepherd and faithful servant of God's people, I believe one thing that can bless the body of Christ or certainly hinder its maturity is the gift or the absence of the gift of discernment. When I say "bless the body" I mean that many things are necessary for effective ministry, but few are arguably more necessary than being able to discern or judge questions, proposals, needs, direction and/or requests of those with whom you come in contact. For instance, when someone says that "the Lord told me" to do this or that and they ask you for your opinion, the gift of discernment becomes invaluable in one's spiritual tool box as it guides in confirming or addressing the issue at hand. For example, someone approached me a while back and asked if they could begin a ministry in the church.

Knowing within, that serving people are maturing disciples, I was anxious to comply. However, in seeking understanding or discernment from God as to whether or not the individual was suited for the ministry, I eventually turned down the request because the discerning spirit said that not only was the person not gifted for the work, but also that they would not be effective in that particular ministry.

The gift of discernment is so very necessary for dealing with what I call the *hyperbole Christians*. You know these kind of Christians don't you; they are the ones who say that the Spirit tells them everything to do from when to start their car to how to chew medium-rare, specifically seasoned porter house steak. I'm really not trying to poke fun at these individuals nor would I dismiss the fact that God speaks to us and is often specifically specific when speaking. However, I personally seem to have a magnetic attraction to those of a hyperbole spirit which has ultimately resulted in a deluge of misinformation as well as several Extra Strength Excedrin sized headaches from time to time. We should all be clearly aware that God sends His Word, Spirit, angels, and new revelation in a variety of ways to speak to and address our needs, but I'm going to step out on a limb here, God generally does not need to tell us when we should go to the bathroom; duh. God gave us a mind to think, reason, and process through almost limitless wonderful and often difficult situations. We worship and praise God not only through the lifting of hands and singing of songs, but it's through mindfully and spiritually working with what God has equipped us and has placed in our heads. I would go one step further to say that our God even rejoices when through knowing His will, we are obedient to it without having to ask God, "is this your desire?"

When I want to challenge Hyperbole Christians about their claims that "the Lord told me," I am careful not to argue their position because I'm not always nor should I be privy to what the Lord is saying to them. Yes, I am quite aware of the scripture that says: "Beloved, do not believe every spirit, but test the spirits, whether they are of God; because many false prophets have gone out into the world. (1John 4:1 KJV) I am also acutely in tune with Paul's writing in the second chapter of 1st Corinthians where spiritual discernment doesn't have to be proven by anyone except the one to whom God is speaking. (1Corinthians 2:14-15) However, when my testing of the spirits comes up short, this is the time that God's gift of discernment is an awesome asset because with it, I can respond not only boldly to claims made, but do so with godly integrity.

In a very real sense a discerning spirit helps us speak to the hearts and needs of others, and that same spirit helps us personally know what course of action we should take. There are amazing and arguably limitless assets in having a discerning spirit: soundness of thought, assurance of decisions, clarity in direction, a greater sense of peace, being in one accord with God's agenda and the list goes on. Likewise there are serious challenges and even consequences that can confront us when there is a lack of or an un-discerning spirit. I openly confess that it has been the lack of a discerning spirit which has caused some of my deepest personal pains and unfortunately, my issues have in some respect negatively affected many in my life.

Now let's stop and address a truth before we proceed. The prayer for discernment is not a prayer about being perfect or having all the answers in any given situation. Like anyone, I would love to be right all the time, especially when it comes to my wife where I have the tendency to get it wrong all too often, but let's not go there *and* don't tell her I said that. I am most sensitive (as I'm sure you are) that God uses our mess ups as instruments to teach, correct, draw us to Him, depend upon Him, and yes to humble our sometimes selfishly personal ambitions which have nothing to do with His purpose. *So true*. To be honest, in spite of our mistakes, we are still engaging in at least one of the "wills" of

God; the permissive will, the promotive will, the providential, and even the punitive will. The truth is that because we are *souled* out to the Lord, and by souled out I mean one's mind, emotions, spirit and being are not only surrendered to God but also abandoned to total trust in God, whatever misdirection, miscalculations, or mis-steps that we make, we are still in the will of God, and therefore we're convinced that God is able to turn any mess into a miracle. This being said, the prayer for a discerning spirit is not asking God for perfection but for divine direction, for understanding and even for prophetic insight.

Too many mistakes have been made with good intentions in mind because a discerning spirit was never sought or evident. Too many personal choices have resulted in self-inflicted wounds and in many cases have resulted in others being hurt as well, because a discerning spirit was not evident.
Allow me to share this with you. When my wife and I decided that we would leave Atlanta to assume a

church pastorate in Cincinnati, Ohio, our intentions were good, and we believed we were being led by God. We actually believed that God would use us to plant new seeds of Christian growth and maturity, and in many ways that did come to pass. It is in this truth that we believed that our season away from the spiritual base and family we loved in Atlanta, Georgia, was effective as fresh and sound healing ministry was instituted. However, we did not take into account or *discern* the toll it would spiritually take on us individually or our immediate family that we were leaving behind. I am well aware that the absence or the dispersion of family members can leave one with a sense of forlorn and hurt because of the separation. I am also fully aware that there are the internet, cell phones, planes, trains and even video cams within computers that allow you to see one another at any given time, but none of these technological miracles can take the place and sense of well being you have when you know that you are in walking distance of the arms of those you love. Love is what a true family is built upon, love and connectedness is what our family has and it is what we cherish. You see, it was not an argument, a need for change or the need to flee one pulpit for another that caused such great anguish in our separation, it was the lack of *discernment* that left me insensitive and unaware as to whom we were leaving, and how the separation would ultimately have a negative affect upon all parties involved. It was the lack of a discerning spirit that caused me to underestimate the hurt and even sense of abandonment that we would cause by leaving our children, grandchildren, church friends, best friends, pesky yet necessary associates and so many others. Even at the time of this writing, now three plus years since we returned to Atlanta, I still hear from former church members about how disappointed they were when we decided to leave where we were pastoring.

Yes, hindsight is always twenty-twenty, but some scars cut deeper than others and have a tendency of leaving gaping and festering wounds. This is why praying for a discerning spirit is so important. It places us intentionally in God's presence where a more complete and accurate picture can be revealed versus the myopic desires we sometimes act upon. Let me further say that when seeking discernment through prayer, more care and diligence will be provided to minister to the hurts of everyone involved.

Discernment by definition is known as a gift according to 1 Corinthians 12:10. As one writer stated, "Discernment is an act of wisdom or detection marked by an insight into a person's character by an event that comes through insight that goes beyond the facts given."[5] In the definition provided, there are several key words that help us get a handle on the gift of discernment. They are *detection* and *insight* about character that goes *beyond given facts*. In the Apostle Paul's writing, discernment is the gift which allows one to know or confirm another person's spirit, intent or actions. To say this in another way, the spirit of discernment is

---

[5] Ryken, Leland, Wilhoit, James C., and Longman, Tremper III. Dictionary of Biblical Imagery, An Encyclopedic Exploration of the Images, Symbols, Motifs, Metaphors, Figures, of Speech and Literary Patterns of the Bible. Intervarsity Press, Illinois, 1998. Pg.207

the ability to read between the lines with accuracy. Therefore, having a discerning spirit is the ability to perceive what the Lord is saying or would say about a person's character or the needed insight into a situation that ultimately governs the discerner's course of action.

Now, we should not ask God to give us a discerning spirit so that we can know whether there is a police car around the corner with its radar gun pointed at us so that we could slow up in time enough not to get the ticket; God gave us common sense to drive within limits. But wouldn't it have been awesome, you that are parents must agree here, that while raising our children, it sure would have been great to be able to discern for sure when your child was lying? Sometimes they give themselves away by the audacity of their story, but there are other times that they lied and did it with such beauty and with such an honest face that an academy award should have been given right then and there for the finesse with which they lied. That kind of discernment would have been good, but the discerning spirit that I pray for is much deeper than this.

Because I endeavor to provide pastoral care to many with problems and issues that I must admit at times leave me speechless, it is at those times when I plead and need a discerning spirit. It is not that I am looking for all the answers or would dare to think that I should possess a spirit of omnipotence, but in the sense of not wanting to see people suffer needlessly or even seeking to be a conduit of relief, a discerning spirit would at minimum arm me or you with the insight to formulate and ask the probing questions that might lead those who are in need to some form of resolution or at minimum mental or spiritual buoyancy. Take for instance what happens during pre-marital counseling. As a standard and pre-condition for marriage, I share with the couple at the first meeting that because I am accountable first to God, if my spirit is not in agreement with the marriage based upon what is shared and or upon what I discern, I will not conduct the ceremony. I mean this and have stuck to that pledge to God and the intended couples over many years. However, I have found that based upon my pre-condition that couples have said exactly what they thought I wanted to hear at the cost of sidestepping potentially damaging issues just so that the marriage might be carried out. The problem with this is obvious; they are trying to appease the counselor while minimizing the pitfalls that will eventually surface which may ultimately destroy the marriage. Though I have studied hard over the years, read many books and conducted many pre-marital sessions, I have found that the best of my efforts sometime fall short of the desired intent. However, if there were a spirit of discernment, it would provide me with the insight necessary to at least catch and address any stated or unstated truth up front, thereby potentially exposing for healing any issues that lay beneath the surface. Though I trust in my counseling and listening skills, still a discerning spirit is able to do what the best of training never can.

In many ways I believe this is where we find King Solomon with his request for wisdom and a discerning spirit as shared in 1 Kings 3:9. When God spoke to Solomon in a dream God said to him, "Ask what I should give you." Solomon being a young man with an empire to govern before him did not ask for wealth, fame, a fifty-two inch plasma television, a set of twenty-two inch gold rims on a Chrysler 300, but his request was this: "Give your servant therefore an understanding mind to govern your people, able to discern between good and evil; for who can govern this your great people?" In chapter one on wisdom, we looked at the "understanding mind" or the request for wisdom, but it is that second portion of verse nine that becomes necessary for us to dissect, the plea for the *important* ability to discern rightly and even in godly ways when decisions are made. There are at least three things that we must understand about his request, why he made it, and why we should pray for a discerning spirit.

1st: He loved God

First of all, Solomon asked for a discerning spirit *because he loved God*. Though he would make his mistakes as do all men and women, Chapter 3:9 clearly states that "Solomon loved the Lord." When you pray to God for a discerning spirit it must be for the reasons and benefits that were stated earlier, but the basis must first be because of your love for God. All too often we ask from God based upon our wants and desires. Jesus Christ told us that we can "ask anything in my name" (John 14:14) and that He would do it, but the motivation behind the request must be based upon a love for God that glorifies Him, but that doesn't always happen. Because we love God, we seek to please God; because we love God, we labor and even sweat to glorify, praise and honor God first for who God is, but then for all that God has done. Whether you are in the ordained ministry or you are a new disciple of Christ Jesus, there are arguably fewer greater blessings and inward joy in life than doing what pleases God whom you love. It is because we love and are in love with God, that our requests are based and centered in the affection we have for God. It is because we love God, that our desire is to be molded into His will. It is because we love the One that loves us the best, that the very axis of our thoughts and consent are pointed toward the One we aim to honor. And, as in the case of Solomon who was saddled with the authority of a king or in our case with whatever responsibility we shall bear, loving God through seeking the discerning spirit of God is one of those glorious ways that we conduct our lives with a kingdom agenda in mind. So then when we pray for a discerning spirit, we do so because love for God is our motivator, and when God is the reason, the discernment given always results in a blessing.

2. He knew and recognized his limitations.

Secondly, Solomon asked for a discerning spirit because he recognized and understood his limitations. Remember, Solomon was a young dude, and what was before him was a kingdom of *individuals*, each with their own minds, needs, concerns, petty attitudes and predispositions as to how things should operate in a kingdom. In many ways Solomon did not have a mega but an ultra-mega church, full of everything holy and unholy and then some. Sensing what was before him was an act of wisdom, but wisdom needed a partner to work alongside of it, discernment. When we pray for a discerning spirit, we are openly acknowledging to God that without Him we are incomplete, insufficient, incompetent and otherwise ineffective. When we ask God for discernment, we are praising God through admission of our inadequacies to handle many situations. Whether we have a large Kingdom to govern as did Solomon or just our own family, a discerning spirit is what makes us over comers in spite of our personal deficiencies.

On one hand a discerning spirit is the divine intervention that reveals truth before or during a given situation, but on another, discernment is also necessary once events have already taken place. In other words, sometimes the meaning of events that took place are not understood until well after, sometimes even years after they happened. I am a witness that God will allow us to grow, not just go but grow through an experience for a given season until God determines that the essence of the lesson can be revealed and the pressure of the situation released. Haven't you ever experienced something that you did not understand? You sought guidance, prayed about it, and you may have even gotten mad with God saying something like, "Why did this have to happen" but no answer came? You had to struggle with the why's and the what if's of it all, but one day, an epiphany or as I like to say God dropped a nugget on your spirit and gave you a discerning mind that resulted in that ageless expression; 'Oh, now I get it.' Discernment then is not only necessary before an event; but, as this example shows, discernment is a much-needed companion at any time. *We need it at all times.*

#3 He wanted to operate in the will of God.

There was a third reason that Solomon asked for a discerning spirit. He wanted to operate in the will of God. As one writer said, "Discernment is always to be desired."[6] Anyone who loves the Lord and wants to give the best of him or herself to God always seeks and desires to operate in the will of God. After all, your calling and my calling, your purpose and my purpose, God's ministry through you and God's ministry within me are about God's agenda, not ours. We want to be in the will of God because we are in God's production. As imitators of Christ Jesus, we are living in our roles as disciples whose sole joy and purpose is to adhere to the script that God has written for His creation and for our particular lives. *So true!* We want to be in God's will because God deserves it, God desires it, and God delights in our yielding. That's why Solomon would seek a spirit of discernment because through it, God's will would be experienced by all. Based upon our love for God, our limitations and our

---

[6] Ryken, Leland, Wilhoit, James C., and Longman, Tremper III. Dictionary of Biblical Imagery, An Encyclopedic Exploration of the Images, Symbols, Motifs, Metaphors, Figures, of Speech and Literary Patterns of the Bible. Intervarsity Press, Illinois, 1998.

desire to operate in His will, let's pray for a spirit of discernment:

Father, in the name of Jesus, we first of all thank you for giving us a good mind. We thank You for giving us a mind wherein we are trusted to think on our own based upon Your Word, Your indwelling Spirit, and our faith in You. We thank You for so trusting us to work with people, to help others, to even know the direction we should go because we have been steeped in Your Word, Your revelation, and held captive by the Light that lives within. Yet Lord You know our weaknesses. You know our failures; You know our dysfunctional characteristics; and our personalities that too often get in the way of carrying out the work that You have purposed for us. Based upon these truths, we seek and plead for this day's portion of Spiritual discernment. We don't seek this gift because of any need to impress or a desire for perfection; we don't seek this gift because we are tired of our failures or afraid of making new ones; but Lord we want to do better, and we just want You to be pleased. We want You to so show us and speak to us so that we not only acknowledge the Light of Christ in us, but that we cherish what You have placed before us.

When friends are struggling, give us a discerning mind in order to help them. When the atrocities of the world have betrayed another one of your children, <u>give us a discerning ear in order</u> to be <u>there for</u> them. When someone is dying and their loved ones are fully distraught, give us the compassionate arms to comfort them through a discerning heart that will sense what they need the most. From the simple to the profound we ask for the insight, the knowledge, the awareness to be a blessing unto You and unto all of Your family, O God, especially unto those who deny or have turned from You. And Lord, as we pray this prayer we position ourselves as those who like Solomon ask and faithfully anticipate our soul's need: a spirit and mind of discernment. In the name that we trust, in the name that is holy and mighty, in the name that assures us in victory, In the name of Jesus, Amen.

CHAPTER VI
-THE ANOINTING-

"God's presence and power are resident in the anointing." Mitchell, Mike Q.V.

Praying for God's anointing as a spiritual discipline is to pray for God's empowering attendance through the Holy Spirit. We should pray for wisdom, courage, strength, patience, and discernment, which as already shared are necessary, but it's God anointing that not only empowers but also equips. The term anoint or anointing is mentioned over sixty times in biblical writings with varying meaning, and before we speak about the type of anointing that we should pray about daily, it is necessary to gain some definitional background.

To anoint by simple definition is to smear or rub oil onto a person or thing. In biblical language the anointing involved many applications, those without *religious* connotation and those with *spiritual* connection. The non-religious anointing involved the ratifying of a business agreement, confirming nuptial rites, a pact of friendship between close associates, and the liberation of slaves. In each of these instances to anoint was to seal the deal. But spiritually speaking the term anoint or anointing had diverse applications and purposes. To anoint someone was a sign of official appointment to office as it represented the symbol of God's power upon him or her. To be anointed was observed as a form of God's protection instanced when David refused to harm King Saul even though his own life was in danger because God's anointing was upon the King. To have an anointing or to say that a person is anointed is the observed and felt recognition that God is doing something uniquely through someone. For instance, when you hear someone singing, there is a difference between the person's talented abilities to sing versus someone who sings the same song but what they sing ministers to the heart. In the former, one sings from talent, training and perhaps desire, but in the latter, the person sings from an empowering presence that transforms notes and scales into healing medicine and renewed hope.

As found in Psalm 18:50, God's anointing is what brings the King and his people victory. It represents God's love and a love that extends (one might call it favor) from one generation to the next. The anointing as found in 1 Samuel 10:1-9 is awesomely multifaceted as several things transpire. In this accounting, Samuel anoints Saul as the "ruler over his people Israel." It's because of the anointing that Saul will: reign over, save Israel from the hand of enemies, have prophetic revelation with confirmation, be "possessed" by God so that he would prophecy himself, be turned into a different person," and finally as verse nine says, because of the anointing he will have "another heart." As one writer said, "the anointing of OT Kings is a special symbol of God's provision through the gift of his Spirit."[7] Reading that testimony makes me want to preach right now on the power of the anointing!

---

[7] Ryken, Leland, Wilhoit, James C., and Longman III, Tremper. Dictionary of Biblical Imagery, An Encyclopedic Exploration of the Images, Symbols, Motifs, Metaphors, Figures of Speech and Literary Patterns of the Bible. Intervarsity Press, Downers Grove, Ill. 1998.

Saul's anointing was personal and what God purposed for him in his season of leadership. Wouldn't you desire the same anointing in order to have advantage over your enemies, prophetic revelation and a changed heart? If God did it for Saul, by faith-filled prayer shouldn't we believe that the same kind of anointing given to Saul is likewise available for us as God's offspring?

In Exodus 30:22-38, we see yet another aspect of anointing where God told Moses to make a formula of holy oil or an oil of holy anointing. The oil was a combination of: myrrh, cinnamon, aromatic cane, cassia and olive oil. Other ingredients used to make the anointing oil were: basor, bay, almond, myrtle, cypress, cedar, walnut and fish oils. But in this text, Moses was told to create the oil that would be used to anoint the tent of meeting, ark of the covenant, the table, utensils, lampstand, and the priests in order as verse 30:29 says, that "they may be most holy, and whatever touches them will become holy." (NRSV) In this anointing, it is first of all transitory entities (tents, tables and lampstands) that are transformed from ordinary into holy instruments or vessels. These articles through the anointing are now in a new state of being as no longer ordinary, but are now altered (if you will) for Godly purposes. But not only are these earthly props transformed into something holy, meaning in this case set apart for God, but also used on wood and upon material that is portioned onto the priests, and as the scripture tells us, they also became holy vessels unto God.

Transformation

Several things are transpiring in this text and are necessary for our understanding. First, God's anointing is about transformation. It is the anointing that moves, shifts, alters, changes, modifies, redirects, and molds items but more importantly *people* into disciples that they are called or destined for even before their birth. It is the transferring and transforming nature of the anointing that lifts us from worldliness and immerses us in the transforming waters called holiness. The tent was transferred from props and material into a holy sanctuary; the ark became not merely a containment of Holy words but also a place where the bread of life existed; the table became a symbol of the prophetic place of remembrance where the ultimate sacrifice would be remembered; the utensils became precious tools for ministry; the lamp stand became a light unto a new path; and the priests became vessels to be used by the living God. Because of the transformative nature of the anointing, it becomes the instrument which gives clarity to confused minds. It is the anointing that reveals a fresh and glimmering light where darkness once had a stronghold; it is the anointing that causes the simplistic to become the profound; it is the anointing that arrests the mundaneness of life and redirects it into abundant living; and it is surely the anointing that allows us to see and experience God as we have our being according to His use of us. Understand this, all of the church's outreach initiatives, ministries, programs, planning, preaching and not to exclude praise and worship are destitute and perhaps dead without the transforming work of the anointing. In fact, the greatest of worship celebrations are rendered to clanging cymbals and chaotic noise when the anointing of God is missing. That's why we pray for it, for we like the priests and even dare I say the tables, tents and utensils want and need change, newness, and transformation. <u>We need God's anointing.</u> *Daily*

#2 Truth & Teaching

Secondly, when asking God for a fresh anointing, we are asking God for a spirit of truth and teaching. According to 1John 2:20, believers are told this: "But you have an anointing from the Holy One, and all of you know the truth." (NIV). Then in verse 27 we are told: "As for you, the anointing that you <u>received from Him abides in you, and so you do not need anyone to teach you.</u> But as His anointing teaches you about all things, and is true and is not a lie, and just as it has taught you, abide in Him." John first of all tells us that the anointing gives the believer the <u>ability to discern truth from fiction.</u> John is cautioning the church against those false teachers who would share a gospel that is anti-Christ in nature. His letter is purposed toward not only warning the Christians of deceitful teachings, but it's charging them to affirm within that they *have* a Spirit of truth that reveals and confirms what they need. It is the anointing then that has the power of dissecting and then dismantling what is heard or presented in order to discern right from wrong. In essence, the anointing according to John is what gives the believer godly consciousness to see, hear and discern beyond what is presented in order that truth may be known. But then, not only does the anointing uncover truth, but it also becomes our teacher. It is the anointing that should be called upon every time we open the word of God so that revelation and understanding might come. It is the anointing that allows the counselor to not only understand theorems and philosophies of human behavior, but also teaches the counselor when to apply it for the purpose of ministry to the counselee. It is the anointing (and preachers will get this) that causes the preacher to change the message in midstream as the Lord reveals a new and fresh perspective to a waiting and spiritually thirsting congregation. So then, we pray for the anointing because we require truth and the ability to recognize it as well as to be taught what we most need.

One of the key purposes for the anointing is so that God can use whatever and whomever for service. In fact, laced throughout scripture is the idea of anointing for the purpose of service. To share this truth, we will look at two sets of passages. First, turn to the book of Exodus 40:9 where the completed Tabernacle and the priests are being prepared for service. First of all verse nine says: "Then you shall take the anointing oil, and anoint the tabernacle and all that is in it, and consecrate it and all its furniture, so that it shall become holy." (NRSV) Before we dissect this passage, it is time that we share this truth: it is not the oil in and of itself that causes the tabernacle and its various items to be transformed into something holy; it is the Holy Spirit of God that makes it all happen. In fact let's make it plain. The anointing is only possible and thoroughly permissible because of the Holy Spirit. We can take all the spices, oils and herbs, pray over them, dance in front of them and rub them on bodies, door-posts and on the sick and lame, but nothing happens without the Holy Spirit. To press this further, when the tabernacle and its contents were anointed in order to become "Holy," the holiness took that nature only because the Holy One's presence was in the anointing oil. It must be clear that when calling and praying for the anointing, we are calling upon the presence, performance, and perfecting nature of the Holy Spirit to make its self known. You will recall that in Exodus 30:29 the priests were anointed and consecrated, (and the two are used synonymously at times) "that they may be most holy; whatever touches them will become holy." The only way that the priests became holy was through God in the Holy Spirit, and the only reason what they touched became holy was because what had touched them was holy, the Holy Spirit.

But now as we look at Exodus 40:13-15 we see the reason for the holiness. God instructed that the people were to, "put on Aaron the sacred vestments, and you shall anoint him and consecrate him, so that he may serve me as priest. You shall bring his sons and also put tunics on them, and anoint them, as you anointed their father, that they may serve me as priests: and their anointing shall admit them to a perpetual priesthood throughout all generations to come." Understand this truth from these passages, the entirety or fullness of the anointing is purposed that God will be served. If the anointing oil is placed upon the sick, it is so that God will be served through our faithful obedience, and if it be God's will that the sick will be made well. If we are given a revelation from God and the anointing to carry out what was revealed, we do so with effectiveness and efficiency because we are serving God. God equips and empowers His own through the anointing not for personal pleasure, performance or the applause by others, but that we may be used as servants unto

Him. Aaron's anointing was clearly purposed for serving God "as a priest." His sons who were also brought before the Lord were likewise purposed as "perpetual Priests" for the service of God. In the language of the King James translation in verse 15, Aaron and his sons were anointed for the purpose of "ministering" unto the Lord. It is perhaps this word "minister" that speaks volumes to the reason for the anointing; we are called to minister unto God. What gifts we have are because of the anointing and enactment through the Holy Spirit; what successes we have in service are because of the anointing and our hearts turned toward ministering unto God. Further, our desires, hopes and passions gain merit and relevance because of the anointing that centers our being toward the sincerest desires of the heart to minister or serve God.

There is one other place where we find that the anointing was for the preparation of service or ministering to God, and it is found in our Lord and our Savior Jesus Christ as recorded by Mark 14:1-9.

Though the testimony records a remorseful woman coming to Jesus and anointing His head and feet, though it records outrage by the onlookers that the cost of the oil could have been used for other purposes, and though that outrage would be directed at Jesus for daring to claim forgiveness of sins, it is in verse 8 that we find additional revelation to this story. The scripture says: "She has done what she could; she has anointed my body beforehand for its burial." Anointing here means at least three things: it means that a person is being set apart or specifically recognized as holy and consecrated; it confers authority or again recognizes the authority of (in this case) Jesus the Christ; but thirdly, anointing prepares the individual for service. To this last point we turn, for in the anointing of our Lord and our Savior, His very being is positioned and prepared as the instrument of ultimate service, dying for the sins of the world. Though this anointing is literal, yet the symbolism of preparation and dedication unto service is undeniable.

It is in this truth that our souls, my soul cries out in prayer daily, "Lord anoint me!" Don't you want God to use you? Don't you need truth and teaching, understanding and discernment, revelation and to be of service to the Lord? [Daily] This is why we should pray for God's anointing, for we are praying that God's Spirit will fill us. We are calling for a fresh rubbing or smearing on of the Holy Spirit that will transform our ways, make us holy, make us useful objects of service. We pray not only for the protection that comes from the anointing of the Holy Spirit, but for the mind's, soul's, and body's increase to experience God in a new way so that His glory will rise and shine through us all to His glory. We pray for God's anointing because some wilderness journeys are so debilitatingly painful that without the anointing we would otherwise simply slip and fall under the burdensome weight of the journey. With these truths in mind, let's pray:

Gracious and merciful God, we acknowledge again and forever how much we need You. We need Your radiating Word, we need Your Shechinah presence, we need Your touch, we need to rest our weary souls upon Your breast, and Lord we need Your anointing. It is Your anointing that cleanses our minds and renews our being. It is Your anointing that takes the fear out of living and gives us the courage of knowing that we're captured in Your arms of love, compassion and protection in all our directions. Lord, it is Your anointing that helps us see, hear, think, do, react, claim, stand, praise, worship, and taste and see that You are good and the soul's delight. Because there are so many needs in this world, because there are so many in need of the Light of the World, because so many have only waded in the shallows and not pressed into the deep, we ask for the anointing to be used by You to draw people unto You. We ask Lord that our hands, eyes, ears, lips, thoughts, desires, our character and everything about us be transformed through the anointing into the tools of Your work so that others might see You and receive their anointing. Abide then Lord in our prayers as we abide in You. Incline thine presence and perfecting power within us for this day's journey and tomorrow's inheritance. Anoint us Lord, anoint us Master, anoint us Holy Spirit; Amen.

CHAPTER VII
-LOVE-

"And if I have prophetic powers, and understand all mysteries and all knowledge, and if I have all faith, so as to remove mountains, but do not have love, I am nothing."

1 Corinthians 13:2

When it comes to asking God for a spirit of love as a daily aspect of our prayer life, the question might well be asked, why do you pray for something that God has already placed within especially if you have given your life to Christ? In other words, since I believe in Jesus Christ as the revealed revelation of God's love, doesn't the mere association with and through Jesus provide unto me a loving spirit? Let me take it one more step, since one is growing in maturity based upon a deeper and expanding intimacy with God, wouldn't a spirit of love be a natural characteristic or component of ones new life in Christ? The answer is yes and it's no. Yes ones relationship in Christ finds its underpinnings in the reality as John so eloquently quoted that, "God so loved the world" (John 3:16 NRSV) and since God loved and loves us so completely, believers by acknowledging and claiming that love from God, likewise should mature in a spirit of love for others. And yes, to desire and maintain ones belief that "nothing can separate us from the love of God in Christ Jesus" (Romans 8:39 NRSV) is not only to possess a soul affirming belief of ones whole care through Christ but also to desire a loving character for living based upon the example of God's passion for us through the Son. I mean this. Because of our intimate and passionate walk and desire for God, our life does go through a transformative process of being cleansed from the bitter experiences that are a part of life as it simultaneously becomes renewed with a right mind and spirit not only for God, but also for self and ultimately for others. Love ought to be our hearts' testimony *because* we are so well loved. Love ought to be our passion as we relate to the revealed truth that God passionately cares for us daily, and love ought to be not only the outward expression of our inward change, but that which gives us unparalleled and uncompromised joy.

Because Christians are called the "Body of Christ," our collective but specifically individual lives take on spiritual transformation - a likeness to the One who lives within - so that God's love becomes our very nature and that which our being is drawn to.

But now let's be real honest because all of us are still under spiritual construction, under our own strength it is hard to love everyone. We are still being shaped, molded, fashioned, and spun on the Potter's wheel as we are maturing into a "holy" other as the body of Christ and temple wherein God's Spirit dwells. However, it's because we are they who are *still in process* regarding our spiritual formation that we have not achieved and in many ways lack the spiritual understanding to love some people and even sometime ourselves. Most of us, if we were God, because we do not operate in a perfected and prophetic spirit of love, would wipe out those individuals who wound and rape young children; tell the truth now. Most of us would blot out from existence those who would plot and carry out acts of terror and destruction upon the innocent and defenseless of this world. Most if not all of us - if we were God - would be fed up with the sometimes inhumane treatment that pandemically plagues this globe where due to sheer indifference toward the sacredness of life great atrocities are allowed to continue to take place. For every holocaust, humankind has proven itself terribly inadequate. For every act of slavery, brutality, act of genocide, drive-by shooting, selling of young boys and girls for sex and profit; for every predator that preys upon the uneducated or elderly; or for every act that victimizes through swindling another individual out of their life's pension, we have fallen short, and if we were God based upon *our* perception of love, there would be few people if any left on earth to give us glory. Even the Psalmist in his meditation expressed his incomplete understanding of God's way by saying: "<u>O that you would kill the wicked, O God, and the bloodthirsty would depart from me- those who speak of you maliciously and lift themselves up against you for</u>

evil." (Psalm 139: 19-20) Though the Psalmist speaks poetically and from a sense of outrage at people's indifference toward God, he still expresses human and vengeful anger toward those who are evil, and in this confounding statement of the Psalmist, someone is being condemned. Humankind has proven itself over its time of existence of being prone to anger which results in retribution and rage, as well as clearly being too impatient to trust in the merits of love's reconciling and healing abilities. Howard Thurman said it so succinctly: "We have failed to love where it was clear that to love was a necessity of the mind and of the heart."[8]

Only a loving God with inscrutable love, wisdom, providence, and divine understanding would allow what takes place in the days in which we live, and in fact, the days that all people have lived. Only a love that's far beyond our capacity of reason and spirituality would allow a creation to continue existing without knowing and understanding the

---

[8] Thurman, Howard. The Centering Moment. Friends United Press, Richmond, Indiana, 1990.

possibilities that are inherent within the creation. And no doubt that's the joy of growing in relationship with God; we gain the privilege of learning to reason, think, give, forgive and yes love like God, and that's exactly why we must pray for a spirit of love. It's not that we don't love and there aren't those that we love with unbounded energy and sincerity, but what I pray for is an increase of spirit that will give me/us that *"in-spite-of"* love ethic. That is, because loving is a way of living or shall I say loving is life, I pray for a spirit of love because the more love I have first of all for God, the greater life itself takes shape in living. The more love I have for God in abiding relationship means that I am or we are peering into the depths of His wisdom and being shown the mysteries of His inner beauty and character. The more I see God, *yes!* experience God, and watch God at work, the more I see life and its purpose; therefore, I become love.

I believe (like you) that life must be about much more than merely existing. Existing day to day in mundane mediocrity is not only a pathetic practice in futility, but it's also a barren existence and inescapably an offence to God. Paul wrote: "love is patient; love is kind; love is not envious or boastful or arrogant or rude. It does not insist on its own way; it is not irritable or resentful; it does not rejoice in wrongdoing, but rejoices in the truth. It bears all things, believes all things, hopes all things, endures all things," (1 Corinthians 13: 4-7 NRSV) which means so many things, but at minimum loving is life because life finds purpose through loving. How else does one put up with the foolishness of those who cause division? It's through patient love. How else does one conduct reconciling ministry? It's through a love that's too compassionate to see anyone slip or fall. How is it that one rejects envy, boasting, arrogance and rudeness and still ministers to the individual? It's through an inner love that has learned to accept people regardless of who they are, recognizing that God poured out that same kind of love for each of us. Love doesn't have to insist on its way because it knows The Way; it need not be irritable or resentful. For what?... God is taking care of all needs. That's why through love, one rejects the sin but never the sinner and is therefore able to put up with all things because love is life.

But then in verse eight of 1 Corinthians 13, Paul helps us with another truth about love; "it never ends." How can what is the charter of God end? Think about it, doesn't the fact that we are alive today prove that love cannot fail? Love is with us, love is for us, love is in us, love protects and covers us, love ransomed a salvation for us, and love gives us reason for living. Love doesn't end when we are denied; it doesn't end when we are at a loss for words; it can't end because the marriage became a ship-wrecked disaster (the marriage may have ended but love is still alive), and love doesn't end when we act unlovable, for we are again promised that "*nothing* (emphasis mine) shall separate us from the love of God in Christ Jesus." (Romans 8:39 NRSV)

Love is what Paul sought to describe yet so much more. Praying for more of the sweet nectar of love equips us with a necessary armor to experience life as well as endows us for every battle we face. Though scripture admonishes us to put on the "whole armor of God, the belt of truth, shoes of peace, breastplate of righteousness, shield of faith, helmet of salvation, and the sword of the Spirit," (Ephesians 6:14-17) one weapon that no Christian soldier can leave home without is the offensive and defensive armament of love. The reason is because when we love, when we live love, when we desire love and desire to love what appears sometimes unlovable, God uses love as a transforming mechanism to draw us into our inner and truest nature, and yes, even the image and character of God.

Catherine di Giacomo di Benincasa better known as Catherine of Siena provided a compelling perspective about love as she believed it expressed from the mind of God. She writes: "When my goodness saw that you could be drawn in no other way, I sent him to be lifted onto the wood of the cross. I made of that cross an anvil where this child of humankind could be hammered into an instrument to release humankind from death and restore it to the life of grace. In this way he drew everything to himself: <u>for he proved his unspeakable love,</u> and the <u>human heart is always drawn by love</u>. He could not have shown you greater love than by giving his life for you. You can hardly resist being drawn by love, then, unless you foolishly refuse to be drawn."[9] Whew, what truth! God draws us to revelation, relationship and the authenticness (my word) of life through God the Son. <u>Not only does God draw us in by the most piercing and agonizing mode of a life and blood sacrifice, but this love is so deep that no wood, no nails, no hammering nor any instrument of death could intercede or interfere with the grace</u> of <u>restoring that which was at a total point of decay;</u>

---

[9] Foster, Richard J. and Smith, James Bryan, Ed. Devotional Classics, *A Renovare' Resource For Spiritual Renewal*. Harper Collins Publishers, 2005. Pg. 265

us. As she suggests, we have the tendency and even propensity of being foolish with love, but when God through Christ reveals the greatest love unto us for us, who in so many ways don't deserve the sacrifice, how can we resist the call and example of God to learn to love like God? How can we or shall I ask, how dare we refuse to see the true radiance of life by refusing to pour our own personal sacrifice into the mold that makes life living; love?

In one of Dr. Martin Luther King's addresses regarding the debate on violence versus non-violence, his writings shared a most powerful perspective of the type of love that I and we should pray for simply based upon human necessity. He writes: "I believe firmly that love is a transforming power that can lift a whole community to new horizons of fair play, good will and justice… Love is our great instrument and our great weapon, and that alone."[10] Love is *the* transformative instrument of God. It moves us to see beyond physical

---

[10] Foster, Richard J. and Griffin, Emilie, Ed. Spiritual Classics, *Selected Readings for Individuals and Groups on the Twelve Spiritual Disciplines.* Harper, SanFrancisco, California, 2000. Pg. 280

limitations, hear beyond what's spoken, and even to press closer towards the withdrawn arms of those who don't want to be embraced. Love transforms our very character, our hopes, our desires, our expectations; love transforms our lives because love is life. When our lives are controlled and transformed by love, we then *become* the transforming ambassadors of God engaged in a holy mission with the authority of the Holy Sender to impart healing, wholeness and hopefully salvation.

And yes, love is a weapon. Love shoots down anger by compassion; it pulls the rug out from under those who stand against its principles by saying, "I will not be turned back!" Love forgives not only self, but forgives the one who cares less that they are forgiven. Love tells evil to take its best shot, it tells apathy and indifference that it must change addresses, it demands we battle beyond color, race or ethnicity; it hears and takes the blows of divisiveness against it yet applies the healing glue that draws individuals back to a place of

[margin note: Love does this]

reconciliation. Love is the soul's defense that causes us to ascend higher than any degrading spoken criticism. Love is the tool used to promote anyone and in fact everyone for the sake of helping him or her find and even accept his or her divine worth. Love does not see boundaries or failures; it sees needs. It responds to the desperation of a soul crying out for understanding even when that soul has committed a most despicable act. It beckons and shouts louder than the abusive needles and the addictive tendencies proclaiming that healing is yet available through the God of love.

Stevie Wonder in a song a while ago shared these interesting words: "Love's in need of love today." The essence of the message is that in too many arenas, love is sometimes a distant cousin only called upon to meet sensual needs or narcissistic desires. Well, the kind of love that we should pray for on a daily basis is a love that not only knows it is needed, but also knows it is secure in the knowledge that love is the only way of life and the only answer to life. It's with this truth that we hear the words of scripture saying that "if I do not have love I am nothing." Hear what is written, "if I don't have love, I am nothing." Think of the implications of this truth. We are told that if we have all the money in the world, investments, 401K's stocks and bonds but do not have love, we are beyond bankrupt. It says that if we sing with perfect pitch and can reach scales that marvel the greatest maestro but do not have love, we can never minister to people, we just sing notes. If I pastor a mega church, tout a biggie-sized choir (sorry, couldn't resist that), have the ultimate missionary board and the most eloquently conceived mission statement yet do not have love, the church is disfigured, dysfunctional and deficient to say the least.

The text says without love "I am nothing." The last time I googled the definition of the word nothing it meant: no quantitative value, insignificant, worthless, no thing, but also no part or no portion, and since we are speaking spiritually here, by definition no love means having no portion with God. If we have no portion with God, what do we have? If we have no portion or connection with God, we have no purpose, no Sovereign, no intercession, no need for prayer, no inheritance and therefore no life. What a pained, pitiful, pernicious life there is without God, not to mention impossible. Since we find our being in God, since God is not only molder and Creator, and since we are made in the image of God, His image of love must be our highest calling. That's why I pray for love every day. I want to experience the depths of compassion that God has for us. I want to be able not only to see the good in every man, woman, boy and girl, I want not only to be able to see the good in every man, woman, boy and girl, but also to share that goodness with them and if possible, help facilitate the best in them as they pull out the best in me. I want God's kind of love as a Pastor, husband, father, grandfather, friend and saint so that I don't lose patience, can sit with those who are grieving or have fallen, empathize and not criticize the substance abuser, forgive when attacked for unfounded reasons, and yes, because of the love I have for God, keep pouring myself into study/prayer/fasting/worshipping so that I will not only grow in relationship with God, but so that I will be a better servant of God. I want to love because I want to share Christ no longer as a means to increase the size of the church (honesty is good), but to do so to increase the Kingdom of God's presence in this world.

Yes, I pray for a spirit of love. I pray for love because even with wisdom, strength, courage, patience, discernment, and the anointing, I am convinced that without love the actual air I need for breathing is missing. I pray for that never ending power that makes life livable. I pray for that character of God that is not put on like an overcoat, but is desired and accepted as my soul's high caliber and purpose. I pray for love to know God even more. So then, let's pray:

With all my heart O great and merciful God I bow to praise and give You thanks. Thanks for the charter of Your love that is unceasing, unyielding, and unselfish toward us, your children. Thank You for meeting us at every point of need, for hearing every single plea, and for watching over every step we take. Today dear Lord I pray, we pray, that You will show us how to love. Teach us how to love. Teach us how to sacrifice out of love. Reveal to us more and more the depths and mysteries of your love. God, You know we need more love. You know we need to love You more in order to love ourselves so that we can love one another. You know and we are realizing more each day that without love our lives are incomplete and otherwise a chaotic mess. We recognize the truth that we have been ignorant with our love, for too often we run to love only those who will in turn love us while denying those who are pleading, even screaming for love.

We have at times directed too much love toward our comforts, our way of religion, and our personal preferences while denying those who are hungry, thirsty and without clothes that stand right outside our door. We have O Lord made love our slave as opposed to becoming a slave to love; forgive us. Therefore God, we seek more love today. We seek more of Your presence, Your touch, Your revelation and truly Your Spirit so that we may love in a way that celebrates You and brings added meaning of life to us Your children. We press into Your presence God, asking for a filling that creates a new person that is never afraid to reveal the love we have been shown and the love we are called to share. We lay down our lives today so that love will pick us up, never deny us, and draw us to our spiritual destiny. We ask these prayers in the name You chose while revealing Your love. We ask in the name that took our loveless selves to the cross and nailed them into oblivion. We ask in the name of Jesus, the love of our soul, and in that name we pray; Amen.

CONCLUSION

"But as it is written, 'What no eye has seen, nor ear heard, nor the human heart conceived, what God has prepared for those who love Him.'"
- 1 Corinthians 2:9 NRSV

There are several truths of which I am certain; first of all that God is. God is all that the sacred Word describes God to be: loving, just, righteous, holy, merciful and full of grace to just scratch the surface. God is sovereign as God needs no board of directors to agree to His decisions, nor does God need any advice on how the script of history (His-story) should be written. God is obvious yet so mystic that He is mysterious, a relentless lover who pursues us with passion yet One whom we must ever strive to encounter. God is, of this there is no doubt. There is a second truth; God loves us, of this I am convinced. We are cared for, fussed over, shielded, protected, forgiven, provided for, and again, loved in more ways than the mind can conceive. How else can we express the character of God, not only as a lover because of His sacrifice in the person of Jesus

Christ, but also in the One who continually witnesses our thoughts and actions yet continues to provide our needs. God must be that mad lover who is so fixated on us that in spite of wars, drive-by shootings, genocide, racism, generational greed, sexism, abusive consumerism which fixates us not on the Provider but the provisions, and much more God still keeps the sun doing its thing, keeps the air flowing to all parts of the earth, provides the rain to water parched earth and throats, and gives life another chance to turn from its own destructive tendencies and live for Him. As the Psalmists asked: "what are human beings that you are mindful of them, mortals that you care for them?" (Psalm 8:4- NRSV) I'll tell you who we are; we are those who are loved by God. We are as Henri Nouwen so succinctly said; <u>we are the *Beloved of God*. We are the experiencing and quite necessarily the confessing witnesses that should declare at all times that because "God is for us, who is against us."</u> (Romans 8:31- NRSV)

Though we thankfully give praise that God is and that God loves us there is this third truth, we will experience seasons of wilderness in our lives. Yes, our loved ones will get sick and they will die even after having offered the most profound of prayers. Yes the home that we were blessed to have cannot only catch on fire, but it can absolutely burn to the ground. Yes, the one that we called our soul mate decided that we had gotten too fat, skinny, sickly, or just simply that he or she got tired of us and decided to head in a younger direction thereby breaking our heart. Yes, we as the beloved of God are they who will wake up one mid-Spring day just to discover that the rains have fallen so hard that our basements have flooded, and the whole city is underwater, and every possession we once owned is now lost in water damage or simply washed away by the floods. And yes, we thought we clearly heard from God only to find out that the voice we heard was not God's but a product of our own unresolved fears or anxieties which caused us to follow a path that led us head and heart combined into the outer reaches of the wilderness.

Wilderness experiences are real. That's why prayer is so absolutely essential. As Richard Foster suggests, where there is no prayer there is no *communion* with God, there is no *contemplation* of the depths of God's purpose and being, there's no *cooperation* in His planning and will and lastly, there's no *change* while in the wilderness.[11] That's what prayer does. It draws us in communion to sit at God's feet to be filled by a manna that only God can serve. Prayer causes us to think beyond our personal wishes and wants to see that there is a much greater picture and panacea that God has in mind for us. Prayer allows us to cooperate in what God has prepared for this world and for our lives as part of the purpose for which we were sent, and prayer changes us from what we thought we wanted to be into the person that God has scripted and chosen for us to be. Paul quoting Isaiah said and I

---

[11] Foster, Richard. Celebration of Discipline, *The Path to Spiritual Growth*. HarperRollins, San Francisco, California, 1978,

will paraphrase: we have not seen, we haven't even heard and our minds have yet to get a real clue as to what God has prepared for us because we love Him. Loving on God is the spiritual stimulus for praying to God. It's because we love God that God, according to Isaiah and Paul, in turn begins to unfold before us the depths of His wisdom, strength, courage, discernment, patience, anointing and His love for us. These seven spiritual prayer tools for handling wilderness times, Wisdom, Strength, Courage, Patience, Discernment, Anointing and Love are perfectly and preciously prepared for those who have a heart for God and who love God.

My prayer is this, because some journeys are far more thorny than others, when we pray the WASACAPADLA prayer, what we are doing by faith is building up our spiritual reserves in Christ as a defense and shield before *and* during wilderness experiences. When we pray for *Wisdom* we don't ask God to necessarily deliver us from the inhospitable surroundings of suffering, but for God to yield unto us the holy insight on how to maneuver and overcome. When we pray for *Strength*, we pray that in spite of the gale forces of adversity that try to knock us off our feet, simply knowing the sustaining presence of God with us will give us the strength to withstand the most violent of winds. In fact let's take that statement where it needs to be. When we pray for strength. We ascend to the truth that it's God's strength that is doing the sustaining, or as the writer said, "not by might nor by power but by My Spirit saith the LORD of hosts." (Zechariah 4:6 KJV) When we pray for *Courage,* we seek not a living deficient of difficult circumstances, but a countenance that walks by faith and not by sight in spite of difficulties. We pray for the courage like Peter who admonished believers to "not be surprised at the fiery ordeals" (1 Peter 4:12) that come in life as if something strange were happening. But that we would have the courage to say with conviction "bring them on because I know God has my best interests at heart." When we pray for *Peace*, we're not praying for the absence of adversity or strife, but that His Spirit equips us with the assurance "that nothing shall separate us from the love of God in Christ Jesus," (Romans 8:39- NRSV) and that that promise of His assuring presence births peace in our souls.

When we pray for **Discernment** we're not looking for personal gain or advantage over our enemies, but we ask for the ear to hear what can be used to glorify God. As Dr. Robert Smith said so well, when we glorify God we do that "which makes God look good."[12] So then, when we ask for discernment it's not only to assist, understand and direct our actions, but ultimately that what is given by the Holy Spirit, will cause us to make God look good. We pray for **Anointing** because we realize that the best of what we have to offer is expected from God, but likewise we realize that without the touch of God on our best, there is no ultimate good that shall be done. And finally, praying for a mind, heart and

---

12 Smith, Robert, Jr. Doctrine That Dances, *Bringing Doctrinal Preaching and Teaching to Life*. B&H Publishing Group, Nashville, Tennessee, 2008.

spirit of **Love** makes everything done, prayed about and hoped for complete. Everything we do, our praise, our thoughts, our relationship, the ministries given and the mission to be done must be shaped, filled and covered in a Spirit of love.

Finally, the type of prayers that utilize these seven tools or principles are not for those who simply want things, but it is for those who are serious enough through disciplined prayer to seek a deeper intimacy with Christ than rote liturgies and creedal statements can provide, though they have their place. These seven strategies are ultimately intended to lead towards developing a deeper relationship with God. They are beckoning to God to draw us nearer in order to steep us in the encounters of His love, for His glory and for whatever wilderness that is or is to come.

BIBLIOGRAPHY

Butler, Trent. Brand, Chad. Draper, Charles. and England, Archie., Editors. Holman Illustrated Bible Dictionary. B & H Publishing Group, Nashville, Tennessee, 2003.

Foster, Richard J. and Griffin, Emilie, Ed. Spiritual Classics, *Selected Readings for Individuals and Groups on the Twelve Spiritual Disciplines*. Harper, SanFrancisco, California, 2000.

Foster, Richard. Celebration of Discipline, *The Path to Spiritual Growth*. HarperRollins, San Francisco, California, 1978,

McWilliams, Warren. Quick Verse Media, Version 5.0, 2005.

Nouwen, Henri. Spiritual Formation, *Following the Movements of the Spirit*. HarperCollins 3-books, EPub. Edition, May 2010.

Ryken, Leland, Wilhoit, James C., and Longman, Tremper III. Dictionary of Biblical Imagery, An Encyclopedic Exploration of the Images, Symbols, Motifs, Metaphors, Figures, of Speech and Literary Patterns of the Bible. Intervarsity Press, Illinois, 1998.

Smith, Robert, Jr. Doctrine That Dances, *Bringing Doctrinal Preaching and Teaching to Life*. B&H Publishing Group, Nashville, Tennessee, 2008

Trotter, M. Dictionary of Pastoral Care And Counseling. Hunter, Rodney J. Editor. Abingdon Press, Nashville, Tennessee, 1990.

Thurman, Howard. The Centering Moment. Friends United Press, Richmond, Indiana, 1990.

SCRIPTURE INDEX
Old Testament

Exodus
30:22-38............ 81
30:29 .... 81, 84
40:9 84
40:13-15............. 85

1 Samuel
10:11-9 80

1 Kings
3:5 20
3:9 .... 72, 74
4:29-13 22

Nehemiah
4:10 36
8:10 34

Job
28:28 17
30:29-31 17

Psalm
8:4 103
18:50 80
46:1 34
111:10 19
139:19-20 92

Proverbs
1:7 17
2:6 17
3:13-15 22
22:17-24 17

Isaiah
54:17 9

Jonah
2:7 2

Zechariah
4:6 .... 33, 106

New Testament

Mark
14:1-9 87

Luke
11:1 2

John
3:16 90
14:14 73

Romans
8:3 46
8:28 15
8:31 103
8:39 .... 90, 95
12:2 63

1 Corinthians
2:9 103
2:14-15 66
12:10 70
13:2 89
13:4-7 94
15:58 52

Ephesians
6:14-17 94

Philippians
4:13 36

Colossians
1:11-12 .... 35, 52, 53, 60

2 Timothy
1:7 39

James
1:5-8 ...…………… 22

1 Peter
4:12 107

2 Peter
3:15 62

1 John
2:20 83

4:1 ..….............… 66

CPSIA information can be obtained at www.ICGtesting.com
Printed in the USA
236352LV00001B/5/P